WARNING:
MAY CONTAIN
NUTS

WARNING: MAY CONTAIN NUTS

ABSOLUTELY THE FIRST DEFINITIVE REVIEW OF THE INCOMPETENT, INADVERTENT AND OCCASIONALLY ILLEGAL WORLD OF BUSINESS IN THE NEW MILLENIUM

BARRY J. GIBBONS

CAPSTONE

Copyright © Barry Gibbons, 2003

The right of Barry Gibbons to be identified as the author of this book has been asserted in accordance with the Copyright, Designs and Patents Act 1988

First Published 2003 by

Capstone Publishing Limited (a Wiley company)
8 Newtec Place
Magdalen Road
Oxford
OX4 1RE
United Kingdom
http://www.capstoneideas.com

CIP catalogue records for this book are available from the British Library and the US Library of Congress

ISBN 1-84112-462-1

Typeset in 11/16 pt Plantin
by Sparks Computer Solutions Ltd
http://www.sparks.co.uk
Printed and bound by
TJ International Ltd, Padstow, Cornwall

To my mum
I promise I will still look for a proper job

Merry Christmas Dan.

This guy seems funny
about business and to know
what he is talking about.
Maybe it'll be of me
for perspective.

GR.

'I could have been someone
(but so could anyone)'
Shane McGowan and the Pogues
Fairytale of New York

CONTENTS

INTRODUCTION

Christ it's dark in here. The backlit screen of my laptop is the only illumination available to help me with this piece of solid scholarship. I am sitting on an old wooden pallet, scrunched up next to some old golf clubs, two (very) vintage bottles of port, and seven years of personal American tax records – archived in case Uncle Sam wants to take more than a passing interest in my immediate history.

I should explain. After a decade in the US, I am living back in our English house, in Bedfordshire. It is built on a hill, in which somebody thoughtfully burrowed (extensively) during World War II and built a concrete air-raid shelter. I still use it today, for miscellaneous storage purposes (see above). Today is a bit different. Notwithstanding the fact that it has a wooden door, which may, or may not, stand up to today's weapons of mass destruction, I am in it and typing this for a very sound reason. I believe our world is about to end.

I know I am not alone in this fear, but my reasoning is, I suspect, different from the widespread paranoia sweeping the rest of the planet. Virtually the whole of the population of the US is now grounded, frozen like a deer caught in car headlights. They await Osama BL, and his Taxis of Terror, dropping the Big One. In their minds, it is only a matter of time, and while they are waiting they will fly nowhere and meet no one.

This is not the only mega-threat on the radar screen. Others fear a wayward meteorite will strike the earth, hitting it with a force equivalent to 2,691,865,872 Oasis concerts. Others fear global warming will do the trick, moving far beyond God's original target (to flood and remove Yorkshire) to leave the earth as a few smouldering islands surrounded by steaming black water.

I am not in any of these camps. *It is my belief that Business will now provide all that is needed for the planet to self-destruct.* For thousands of years, commerce of one kind or another has driven the planet forward with the good generally outweighing the (admittedly) extensive bad. Wealth has been created and the overall quality of life improved beyond recognition. In the last century both of these trends have accelerated exponentially. However, when the current CEO of Earth PLC, i.e. God,[1] looks over the Earth's latest dismal annual report He (or She) will despair. He (or She) will see Earth's towering and escalating debt, threadbare liquidity, diminishing replaceable resources and the huge and widening disparity between the double-handful of Fat Cats running it and the millions of pismires[2] being 'run'.

He (or She) will then follow a clearly defined process. First of all, He or She will take a leaf out of Rupert Murdoch's (News

---

1 And here you must insert the name of your own chosen deity – I do not want to offend anyone THIS EARLY in the book.
2 This is a wonderful word – as it's not actually rude. It is a kind of ant-like creature, and you can get away with murder by using it in the middle of a tirade.

Corporation) book and put out a set of trading results for the Earth that indicate enormous 'Net Profits Before Other Items'. This is a new and exciting concept in profit reporting, developed by another Master of the Universe. It is so new and exciting, in fact, that nobody else *knows what it is*, but it enables the media to report a small black figure rather than a mind-boggling red one.[3] He (or She) will then sell their stock before giving out any bad news – trousering an enormous personal gain. They will then call in Earth's auditors, who will imitate a Chinese Fire Drill while they shred every document on the planet. Then, after a short spell in make-up, and with an onion in their top pockets to aid the tear flow, they will announce at a press conference that Earth PLC will be seeking protection from its creditors. *Earth will then be declared bankrupt, and Life, as we know it (Jim) will cease.*

It is imminent, trust me. Why else would I be in my air-raid shelter?

Were there any hints before the great corporate suicide bombings (e.g. Vivendi, Vodaphone, Marconi, WorldCom *et al.*) that should have warned us? Should we have spotted flaws and faults in the system BEFORE the great business SMEFs[4] of today?

I think there were and that we should have.

Let's start with something called a *billion*. Now, contrary to what you may have been taught at school, a billion is not a million millions. It is but a thousand millions. Despite this kick in its knee, the idea of a billion remained rather vague during most of my adult life. It was just too big, and simply too much, to get my head around. It ranked up there with the mystery of infinite space. It was one of those things that confused me – in the same way I get confused when

---

3 In the case of News Corp, August 2002, a 'Net Profit Before Other Items' of $636m actually becomes a reported LOSS of $6.3 BILLION after the 'other items' are added in. Well, if you want to be picky ...

4 I am indebted to Terry Jones – he of Monty Python fame – for capturing the concept of a SMEF (Spontaneous Mass Existence Failure). I can't remember where I read it, but it was his – and if there is a finer way of describing what happened to the likes of Enron, I have yet to come across it.

I read the obituaries in the newspaper. Isn't it freaky how all these people always die in alphabetical order? The idea of me ever possessing a billion was up there with the dream of my beloved Manchester City soccer team winning the Champions League. In short, it was big, confusing and completely unattainable.

It has now assumed a position in modern business life as Chump Change – which may have been where it all started to go wrong.

I once tried to make it real and understandable. I worked out that if you had a coin or note that represented one single unit in value, it would take one person somewhere between three and six days to count a million of them. The variation depended on how many pees you had and if you slept at all. Therefore to count a single billion would take somewhere between *eight and sixteen YEARS*. So, that didn't help to close it down much.

Now then. Consider this. In the first couple of years of the new millennium, Vodafone,[5] the UK mobile phone server, lost market value of about *two hundred billion pounds*. This, of course, is completely beyond all our kens, so I'll try to make it real for you by going through it in bite-sized chunks.

We'll start somewhere else and meander back. During the same period, a Mr Gordon Brown, who happened to be, at the time, the UK politician in charge of our nation's purse strings, made his seven hundredth (by my count) play for the future job of prime minister. Speaking to a hushed Parliament, he announced that he was producing, out of a hat, a financial rabbit that would solve a half-century of underfunding and geometrically increase unsatisfied demand in the British National Health Service. It would cost the taxpayers approximately forty billion pounds.

Aha. The quick ones are ahead of me. So why, you ask, couldn't Vodafone, while plummeting downwards and pissing its billions of

---

5 To all Manchester City fans this is universally pronounced as Vodafonney. It sounds much more effeminate, and suiting to the brand that sponsors Manchester United.

pounds away, deflect those billions – and possibly overfund the new NHS requirement by a multiple of five times? If that could be made to happen, Vodafone investors would be in exactly the same place as they are today, and everybody in Britain would have their own dedicated doctor, nurse and *en suite* hospital bed – just waiting for them *in case they were ever ill*. Easy?

The core of this nonsensical question you have just asked is one of the reasons this book is here now. Just by asking it, you evidence deep confusion, so let me explain why it can't work. You see, Mr Brown spends *real* money – money he gets from taxpayers. He gets a lot of it – those billions again – which is one of the reasons I dab a bit of perfume on my annual tax return. If he's going to do that to me, I figure it's important I should at least make the effort to smell nice.

Now, let's contrast that real money with Vodafone's. *Their 'lost' billions never really existed*. It was, to quote the magnificent Eddy from AbFab, all buggery-bollocks. And Vodafone were far from lonely in first building up this kind of incomprehensible wealth, and then rubbing vanishing cream on it.

So, the first great foundation stone of the new millennium – all those astonishing market capitalizations creating incalculable wealth – crumbled. We learned three lessons. First: Warren Buffet was right – again. Second: you are not a millionaire, much less a billionaire, until you've sold the bloody shares and paid the bloody tax. Third: if it's too good to be true it's because it isn't. Massive lay-offs came around again, huge spending cutbacks were mandated, companies tanked and big pension funds became underfunded. Consumers responded to this crisis by borrowing more. Inspired by TV advertising ('Hey, why not consolidate all your unrepayable little loans into one humungous unrepayable Big Loan?'), with the result that an average American family now has a bigger debt than a medium-sized country in the Balkans.

In the US, a parallel script was unfolding. Enron, the darling of Wall Street, with its metaphoric finger up virtually every US politician's fundamental orifice, went belly up. What was the cost to their investors, employees, pensioners, suppliers and other sundry stakeholders? Another paltry few hundred *billion* dollars. Just as importantly, they chiselled through some more foundation blocks of the world we knew. We thought the personal greed excess of the eighties was gone – but it was alive and well, hiding *just below the surface* in some of these complex global entities. During the year it went under, Enron paid its small executive team a half of one of those billions (that's five hundred million if you've lost me) between them. This figure *excluded* gains from their own stock sales – many of them made at prices they knew would be baloney in weeks. In the staggering case of the company Chairman,[6] some of these stock sales were made *back to the company* so they wouldn't have to be disclosed. These guys, remember, were the gallant few who built the rancid corporate architecture, who fostered the conflicts of interest and who knew of its built-in fault lines. Then, just when we thought corporate governance had hit a new low, on to the stage walked Arthur Andersen, Enron's auditors. The ensuing news broke like a thunderclap – the corporate 'police' were in on it too! More foundations crumbled.

It doesn't help, of course, that the hand on the tiller of the world's biggest economy – the US – is the hand of a dipstick. George Bush Jnr, with the winds of his own country's Falklands Factor in his sails – in his case the war against the Taxis of Terror – found out that he had to pay his debts to the 'supporters' that got him elected. So, just when the planet needs an outward looking, internationally catalytic and eco-responsible US, we get the opposite. Those billions of dollars spent by the US Administration's vested-interest supporters and lobbyists were truly some of the safest-return investments in recent history.

It is my observation that business, today, has a far more powerful impact on our daily lives than government, religion or politics.

6 Don't get me started on this guy. All I will say at this stage is that, if I were Schindler, he wouldn't be on my list.

About half of the world's biggest economies are now corporations. Depending whether you are an Internet freak or visit a lot of supermarkets, you may be exposed to anything from 20,000–30,000 brand messages *a day*. Business remains, for most of us, the source of our prime wealth creation – but it also provides us with many inputs to our personal development. We experience many behavioural patterns, attitudes and values from our exposure to work – some good, some bad and many in between. We also experience relationships, and how to (and how not to) deal with other people. We find mentors and folk to mentor. We learn more from the workplace than we ever learned at school, university and – yes – business school. *But what the early years of the new millennium have shown us is that much of what we relied on is destroying itself.* There can be no pride or comfort in working for one of these soulless one-eyed behemoths – and this can apply to any business with more than ten employees.

So, you see, we don't need Osama or meteors or floods. We are doing a fine job of destroying our world all on our own. Just fine.

Are there any causes for optimism? Well, yes – but they are few and far between. In the UK, Marks & Spencer ended the old millennium illustrating just how fast you can sail a liner into an iceberg. A 'Perfect Storm' mixture – arrogance, myopia, incompetence, adverse competitive conditions, the loopy pursuit of one of those billions in reported profits and all this topped off by having a Chairman called 'Rick' – saw this century-plus old blue chip all but destroyed in less than two years. But the early years of the millennium have seen a fight back – which was somewhat predictable, but at a speed which was not.

Tesco, Amazon, some cut-price airlines, eBay and a few banks showed that there is life after the Dotcom collapse. Some old economy examples, some new – but *it can be done*.

The only other cause for optimism that we will survive into a second decade of the millennium lies with our youngsters. Just as they are showing wisdom way beyond their years in abandoning politics, equally they are abandoning 'career paths' and corporate life sentences. Many of them are embarking on 'Gap Years' that will never end. They communicate with each other via a new language, typed entirely with the left thumb onto impossibly small mobile phone keyboards. They are planning their lives around their soon-to-be-dying-Boomer-parent legacies. And they couldn't give a shit about earnings per share, but they are increasingly taking to the streets to protest against the excesses of unfettered capitalism and alienating governance.

I am too old to don a ski mask. But our only hope lies with them, and I am not overconfident it will be enough. It is important, therefore, as God's auditors seek to shred every revealing document and to destroy all paper trails, that some record exists of the antics and madness of the new millennium business world. That is my task, even if it is written in the dark. The latter fact will also explain, in advance, all typos and incorrect semicolons.

In these 50 or so essays I have adopted the rather unlikely disguise of a bird, skimming the rooftops of the corporate life. I land here, I pause there. I squawk a lot. More than once, as one does, I crap on a carefully chosen target.

Barry Gibbons
Befordshire, England
Email: Gibbonfile1@aol.com

THE EMERALD TIGER AND DAME EDNA

It's probably safe to say it now. Just about. As the late, great Ian Dury (he of the Blockheads) might say: 'It was all bollo, wannit?' All that scaremongering stuff. Eventually, the dreaded Y2K came and went with but a whimper. As my old Latin master might have put it: '*Ars longa, vita brevis*', or 'Big arse, short life'.[1] Which was all rather sad in my book.

A long time ago, a heartless soccer coach described one of my legendary on-field performances as 'banging on a window with a sponge' – and that sums up the passing of the old millennium and the arrival of the new one. This disappointed the wife of a friend of

---

1 It's a long time since those Latin lessons. I may have this translation a bit wrong. But I'm sure you get the picture.

mine enormously as she had laid in endless tins of Spam, gallons of bottled water, about a ton of kindling wood, ten surgical dressings and a not unimpressive Gatling gun.[2]

Personally, I was hoping a couple of things would implode and disappear forever at the passing of midnight on 31 December 1999 – namely Sting and all the world's taxation databases. 'Twas not to be.

We have, however, now had the chance to have a look at the New Century, and you could easily come to the conclusion that it has a face like a welder's bench. Osama BL, of course, has grabbed the early-century headlines, bursting into America's very own kitchen and rattling the whole worlds of religion, politics and business. I was almost deafened by the thunder of sphincters clicking open and shut in the boardrooms of the world, although (as ever) the enlightened found an opportunity in the darkness. I'm referring, of course, to those ailing and failing organizations who were suddenly given a glorious excuse to lay off thousands and explain away crappola performances.

Clinton's gone, of course. The word Clinton comes from the Cantonese *Ton Clin* – which means (literally) He Who Cries With One Eye – but it is a bit sad to see the daft sod now splashing about in life's shallow end. He almost ruined everything, of course, with some crazy last-day-in-office activities – but I suppose we must accept he was terribly concerned about his 'legacy'. He needn't worry. He will be forever known as Shagger.

In politics the left-wingers have continued their move to the centre, and those who occupied the centre have moved to the right – with a lot of nationalist rhetoric masking tawdry protectionism, isolationism and racism. The anti-globalists gathered topspin and continued to confuse the *bollo* off the overclasses where an average employed Western family now, by the way, has no children and 2.7 four-wheel-drive sports utility vehicles.

---

2 These items are now for sale at VERY advantageous prices.

Elsewhere, the early years of the new millennium have confirmed what we should have known all along – that Warren Buffet was right. The dotcom and telecommunications worlds imploded, and wonderful inventions such as 'Operating Profits Before E-Commerce' found their correct place in history (i.e. next to 'Lite' beer). Corporate governance continued its downhill quality trend – with Enron rewriting the science, and their auditors Arthur Andersen (yes, their *auditors* for Chrissakes) looking as though they wouldn't be out of place refereeing pro wrestling ('Whaddya mean, he came into the ring and hit you with a tin chair while I was looking the other way …')

Let's take a quick look at Planet Business at the start of the New Age.

First stop – the Emerald Tiger. I'm writing this bit half-looking at a lovely building on the banks of the river Shannon in Limerick, Ireland. The building dates back well into the nineteenth century when it was a barracks for the British army. It is still called the Strand Barracks building, and it is where my father was born in 1905. Today, it has been converted into luxury apartments to house a few of the country's new executive elite – and I am sure my dad is amused by the whole idea, perched as he is on a cloud somewhere, smiling.

As the Land of My Father, Ireland is a country that is dear to me. I am one of the few people on earth who can cry listening to a Pogues album, but I admit I am no nearer working out the country's crazy paradoxes than anybody else. It is very easy to hate Ireland with every fibre of your being on account of Michael Flatley and *Riverdance*, but that would be unfair. Ireland (the country) recently completed another year as Europe's fastest growing economy. The double digit annual growth rates of the turn of the millennium have slowed down a bit, but property prices have trebled in three years, taxes are being cut, unemployment is low and the place STINKS of prosperity. You cannot go out in the street without tripping over a European subsidy for something.

The Irish economic and business worlds are not the only ones giving off signs of better times emanating from this long-troubled isle.

My father delightfully summed up the problem we Brits had with 'The Irish Question'. It was that every time we thought we had an answer, the Irish secretly changed the question. It may be, however, that an endgame is at last in sight to the political nightmare of the past 40 years. The Republic has – at least officially – withdrawn its constitutional claim to the north. In the north, an Assembly has been voted in by the people for the people. Catholics and Protestants share power in it – power which has been devolved to that Assembly from London. The IRA agreed to explore the idea about talking about a possible meeting to discuss a process that might end in another meeting to discuss decommissioning their weaponry – somehow, sometime, someplace. Then they amazed everybody by starting the process.

Times are good. Ireland looks a bit like a lavatory attendant who has won the lottery.

The country also fascinates me in the context of the changing ideas about branding. There is a school of thought that says that branding has moved away from being product-led – where it was firmly rooted for over a century. It is still about getting distinction in cluttered competitive markets, but that distinction is now less about WHAT you do and more about HOW you do it. You have three variables to deal with – price, specification and the relationship you have with the buyer of your product or service – and it is the latter that is growing in importance in the mix.

It is as though Ireland and the Irish understood this way before the likes of Branson. Compare Ireland, for example, with Wales. As noted above, my father was from the former. My wife is from the latter – and I feel I know both well. The countries, that is. There are many similarities. They both have rugged mountains, picture-book hills, verdant valleys and a beautiful coastline. They both have a powerful literary and musical heritage. Wales, of course, never had The Famine[3] but is no stranger to hard times. In other words, WHAT

---

3 I've always thought this an odd claim to fame. How the hell can a million potato-less people starve when the rivers and seas are TEEMING with fish?

they do is quite similar – but HOW they deliver their offering to the world 'market' could hardly be more different. The gap between their respective effectiveness and efficiency in the 'marketplace' is astonishing. Wherever you are in the world, the Irish 'brand' is present – either through an 'Irish bar' or spiritually through some would-be ex-pats.

Although I yell the opposite at the companies I work with, it is still possible to sustain a brand on bullshit for an astonishingly long time. The grand masters, of course, are the Swiss Army, from whom we may shortly expect a range of hardwood dining furniture and a wine collection. The Irish must have studied them diligently. St Patrick's Day is now almost a worldwide event – but there is no evidence that there ever was such a guy (although an alternative school of thought suggests that there may have been two of them). Guinness is the national drink – but it is now mainly brewed in west London. The Irish 'brand' emblem is a shamrock – which also doesn't exist. The whole thing consists largely of smoke and mirrors.

Ireland's 'brand awareness' must be up there with the likes of Coke and McDonald's – whereas nobody has ever heard of Wales. Which is just fine with my wife – but a bummer for some of the inhabitants who could use an economic goosing.

There are undoubted barriers within the whole island – not the least of which will be the internecine struggles within the north itself, but I have every finger crossed. The Irish, when they avoid the temptations of self-parody, and they *don't* think of themselves as some sort of international brand concept, are delightful. Just delightful. They deserve a golden age.

There are early signs that a federated Europe might just get its act together and overtake the US as the world's prime superpower by the end of the new millennium's first century. Some of the issues that will need to be addressed are already popping over the parapet. Early in the new millennium, in Germany, the mighty Mannesman company were unhappy about the successful takeover bid for them

submitted by (the British) Vodafone.[4] So was the German government. During the bid process, both of them scrambled through the
German and European company law statutes to find a reason to
declare it illegal. The bid, you see, was unsolicited – or 'hostile'. The
Germans, apparently, don't like hostile takeovers.

Now, do me a favour and read that last sentence back to yourself – slowly. That's it, the one that says *Germans do not like hostile
takeovers*. That should go down well in Poland and France. Also in St
Petersburg. I know that we live in irony-free zones today – but does
anything strike you as humbug-ish in Berlin's adopted position on
this?

Now, let's pan the New Age camera WAY down south – to Australia. I grew up with a very stereotyped view of this nation, which
is seemingly untouched by culture or subtlety. One of the funniest
crowd chants I ever heard was from a small bunch of visiting Brits
(a.k.a. 'Poms') at a cricket match between Australia and England in
Brisbane. We Poms were having a hard time at the hands of their
team and crowd, but after a few beers our guys launched into a cho-
rus of 'If your Granddad was deported clap your hands'.

This tiny nation – crowded in the bottom right-hand corner of
the country – suddenly seems as well placed as many 'bigger' names
to face the New Age. Their wines are as good as any. In sport, it is
difficult for the US reader to understand, but the other 95% of the
world's population don't really give a puck about ice hockey, grid-
iron football, basketball or baseball. In the sports the other six billion
people play, in the first years of the new millennium, Australia won
(genuine) world championships at tennis, cricket and rugby. They
also reached the final of the under-17 soccer World Cup, which they
narrowly lost to the more likely Brazil. They have a swimmer, Ian
'The Torpedo' Thorpe, who is unbeatable (seemingly) over any dis-

---

4 This was in the heady days before Vodaphone and much of the international
telecoms industry tanked as it turned out everyone on earth didn't need THREE
mobile phones or 24/7 long-distance Internet access.

tance using any stroke if he chooses to take part. Digger Murdoch's empire dominates the media world. An Aussie, Douglas Daft, has taken over from the beleaguered Doug Ivester at Coca-Cola. Sydney hosted the 2000 Olympic Games, and improved profoundly on Atlanta's one-eyed, tawdry performance. All impressive stuff.

Perhaps Australia's finest current export, however, is Dame Edna Everage. If you go to see 'her', take a small piece of advice from me. Don't sit in the front two rows. She has some glorious 'put down' lines. Asking someone in the audience if they believe in reincarnation, she doesn't wait for a reply but fires in the follow-up: 'Well, you look as though you might have been something once.'

Strangely, on the night I was there, the 'victim' looked nothing like Rod Stewart.

MEDIOCRE, SAD
AND CHEATING:
THE ASCENT OF MAN

For many years now my wife has been immersed in the wondrous world of genealogy. For almost as many years I left her and it well alone, thinking, mistakenly, that it was all about the mysteries of female reproductive organs. Apparently that is another, albeit similar-sounding, science. This one is actually about family trees. Phew.

Once I knew that, there was no stopping me. Within days I had traced the living descendents of Alexander the Great (356–323BC), Frederick the Great (1712–1786) and Alfred the Great (871–900). Out of respect for their privacy, I won't tell you their addresses or phone numbers – but let me tell you who they are and what they are doing.

The seventy-first generational descendant of Alexander the Great has the same given name, but his full name is now Alexander the Mediocre. He works in the 'call centre' of my bank. My bank is one of the world's biggest, and I won't tell you which one it is except to say it has the greatest nickname of any corporation anywhere.[1]

I have been with the bank for about 35 years, and I have reached the stage in life where I qualify for the esteemed title of High Net Worth Individual. If I want to telephone my bank, however, and talk to someone, I have to ring in to a call centre – which I suspect is somewhere in northern India. Before any conversation happens, or I can be put through to someone who knows me or of me, I have to tell Alex the M my mother's maiden name – which is a security code apparently I've agreed. The trouble is I have had a mother and a stepmother, and can't remember which one I gave. The minute I hesitate, I am treated as though they have heard leper bells down the phone.

Here's what I should do to Alex. I *should* tell him to stuff his bank, but I can't be bothered. It will be a pain to relocate my accounts – and all the other banks will be the same anyway. I suspect that this pathetic attitude of mine is the glue that keeps 90% of modern customer relationships alive. In the end there is nobody to blame but us for putting up with this crap.

The seventh linear descendant of Frederick the Great is also called Fred. In his case it is Fred the Saddo, and he has many siblings and cousins. You realize what this is about when you ask him his job.

For thousands of years, people have used a summary narrative of the products and/or services of their labours to describe their jobs (farmer, carpenter, train driver, pizza salesman etc., etc.). On the surface, Fred the S and his siblings all do such work. Their companies provide the world with some sort of product or service. In reality, however, their 24/7 job is to do nothing but manipulate their company's share price. It doesn't matter a fig to them what products and services they market – all that matters is the share price of their com-

---

1 The Honkers and Shaggers.

pany. Their life is a constant flow of spin-doctorship, press releases, overstating revenues, PR and misinformation.

Now, there's nothing new in propping up a share price of a company of course, but the last 20 years has seen stock become a key weapon in mega-acquisitions and executive pay. That changed everything. The result is that thousands – millions – of employees focus on *nothing other* than stuff that will directly or indirectly keep the company stock in some anti-gravitational hover-mode. This is the real Deep Vein Thrombosis that brought down Enron and World-Com *et al*. What a miserable, sad way to earn a living.

Now, Alfred the Great's modern direct descendant is of an entirely different kidney. You can spot it in his name – Alfred the Cheating Bastard. I will tell you exactly where he works – in the finance department of a company called O_2 – previously known as British Telecom. This is my mobile phone service supplier. Cell phones, as you know, are a bit like wire coat-hangers in that if you leave two of them in a cupboard overnight, they breed. So, we now have several of the things, all with this company.

Like many lazy guys, I pay my mobile phone bill by standing order, and just track the total cost as it passes across my breakfast table each month. On one 'low-news' day, however, I read it, out of curiosity, and discovered that I was paying about £2.50 per month, per machine, for something called 'handset insurance'. Now, there are two points to note here: first, the handsets cost nothing, and would cost nothing to replace in a market where suppliers are getting desperate; second, when I checked, it was *quite clear,* in all three contracts, that the provision of handset insurance (or any other optional extras) was EXCLUDED from the signed contract.

What we have here is sinister. Big Al is sitting in his office in O_2, *unilaterally* adding out-of-contracted extras to customer bills – in the hope they won't be noticed. Now, if I contracted to sell someone some timber, and then unilaterally added the price of insurance for it when the contract specifically omitted to do so, and then I took the money anyway, wouldn't I be a cheat? What say you, Al?

When O_2 are caught out, as in my case (and you might want to check yours, right here, right now), they agree to stop it immediately. If you were the one in a thousand that could be bothered to force the issue, I suspect they might reimburse you a few pounds. And why wouldn't they? I suspect this gameplan is netting them millions – and a few pay-offs to keep it quiet would be money well spent.

Alfred has many, many siblings and cousins. There is Alfred the Crafty Bastard, who works for a company called TXU Energi.[2] They have just sent me a nice letter, which informs me (I am not inventing this) that they want to be 'allowed' to 'continue with the improvements we are making to the service we provide our customers'. To facilitate this improvement they will be taking my standing order from my bank 14 days *earlier*. I don't know about you, but I would prefer they worsened my service and took the money two weeks later. Do they think we are idiots? Answer: no. They are relying on our anaesthetized apathy to do nothing, while they trouser two weeks aggregate cash flow. That's a lot of cash across their customer base.

Another cousin, Alfred the Cheeky Bastard, is on the board of Sketchley, the UK dry cleaning chain. They have switched policy – again, probably to help 'serve us better'. What they do is now take your money *in advance*, i.e. when you hand your cleaning in. In effect, they use your money to clean your clothes.

So, there they are – the direct descendants of three of history's great men. One is Mediocre, one is Sad and the other brothers and cousins are Crafty, Cheating and Cheeky. They exist because we, the people, have the power to assassinate them, but we just can't be bothered anymore.

It was Jacob Bronoski who summarized the last few thousand years as the *Ascent* of Man. Not in the case of these guys it wasn't.

---

2 This is another candy-ass brand name change in the utility industry – this time it's the one supplying my domestic electricity.

HOW MANY TEARS ...

I have an increasing admiration for today's teenagers. They are sure-footed and capable. Nothing new surprises them. They are *übernerds*, punks, rappers and amoral. All in one body. They take exactly what they need out of life, and leave the remnants to us. They have invented one of modern life's critical new sciences – *percussive maintenance* – which involves HITTING any piece of technology (e.g. a mobile phone) that doesn't work.

In a recent survey, 92.7% of 18-year-olds couldn't give a shit about any subject on which they were interviewed. They can get the word 'like' into a sentence several hundred times. I spotted (seriously) a recent survey where 68% of those questioned said they had no intention of ever voting, and my heart warmed to see so much sense in those so young.

As a by-product, it is nice to see my own position on voting validated by the newly-adult generation. I have never been able to bring myself to vote for the tedious, lying egomaniacs that purport to represent my interests. My father fought to defend democracy, not what's emerged in its place. So, on one subject at least, I am at one with the generation that has had things pierced that cowardice has enabled me to leave whole.

They are, of course, about to enter the world of business – and they will shape it in new ways. I have always been interested in how social trends manifest themselves, eventually, in business. As families have become less patriarchal, so businesses have become less elitist. As the military became less influential in our lives, we became less formal, first in life, then in business. Women's emancipation has been followed, albeit far too slowly, by their increasing impact in the workplace.

There are a few current trends in society that have not yet hit business. They will duly arrive there in the hands of this new generation. On the surface, the prospect is not enticing – for these trends include the addiction to fatuous statistics and the move to 'zero tolerance'. Following closely behind comes the trend of the increasing 'nannying' role of government, and the widening gap between rich and poor. I think the first of the new trends to arrive, however, will be my special favourite. I call it *emotional incontinence*.

I was born immediately after World War II in the industrial north of England. Yes, yes, yes, we all had long walks to school in the snow, and could barely afford ointment for our polio, but all that hilarity aside, the attitude to trauma and tragedy was markedly different. As a family, we were neither poor nor rich, but it was a dark, tough world. Almost every house had suffered a death or injury in the war. It wasn't a Third World nightmare, but terminal disease was still a big factor. In short, death and tragedy were frequent visitors to most families. I don't know whether it was just a British thing, but we handled it in a very reserved way. We put a diaper over our emotions. It was not the done thing to cry, or emote in public. You handled it stonily, and moved on.

It was with the death of Diana that I realized how much the world had changed. Public grief took on the proportions, exposure and *character* of a Super Bowl half-time show. British people cried on TV. Bernie Taupin took one of his finest lyrics and turned it into cloying drivel, and Sir Elton Candlewind[1] then sold millions of records containing it.

In the US, there are now multiple occasions every year where some fruitcake guns down an office or a classroom. They are always followed by makeshift shrines, teams of counsellors appear everywhere, memorial services are broadcast and everybody weeps on CNN. People seem to seek the spotlight to wail, and not a dark place under their stairs where they can privately come to terms with their grief. Just when you think it can't get any worse, some spotty kid may emerge in front of a TV camera and sing a nauseating, self-written, REM-style dirge, backing himself on acoustic guitar. And there is, of course, the collective seeking of something called 'closure'. At any one time, there are, in my estimation, at least 120 million people in the US seeking this mystic goal.

I think emotional incontinence may become THE first big new business idea for the new millennium. If your company has a mid-sized crisis – let's say like Xerox in the US, or Marks & Spencer in the UK – then I think an *impromptu* shrine of flowers and teddy bears on the pavement, outside the corporate offices, could be quite effective. A team of counsellors could help traumatized shareholders come to terms with their losses. The executives who made the bad decisions that caused the mess could be analysed *ad nauseam* on serious TV documentaries. Where did they go wrong? Did the music of the Eagles have some latent sinister effect? How on earth did their

---

1 I have stolen this name, unashamedly, from *Private Eye* magazine – a source of inspiration and plagiarism for me for about 40 years. It is a far better surname for the man in question than John.

parents (aged 86 and 92) miss the obvious signs? Are there *Gothic* dimensions? Then, a guy from Accounts Receivable could write and perform an acoustic dirge. Media-sponsored hackers could roam through the e-mails of the guilty managers and look for signs that might have warned of pending disaster.

Of course, if it's a REAL disaster, a sort of Enron or Marconi pee-on-your-own shoes mega-SNAFU, the above won't be enough. A full time VP of Closure will have to be employed to help losing shareholders and pensioners dry those tears and find inner peace. And handle the press briefings. A Charity Foundation must be set up immediately, with a website and a logo.

Then, and only then, I think the mark of a really class act would be to bring in an ageing Bob Dylan. Nothing less than a full rework of the lyrics to 'Blowin' in the Wind', would suffice, cleverly (but with sensitivity) working in the company's brand sound bite.

4

REFLECTIONS
FROM TIBET

Almost everybody I know is exhausted from the flu. I too, am tired, spiritually and physically, but for a very different and, I like to think, more worthy reason. Recently, I arrived in the Indian town of Dharamsala, after a 900-mile trek over the mountains from Tibet in the dead of winter. There, we proudly introduced Ugyen Trinley Dorje to the free world. His name alone is worth 400 points at Scrabble. Otherwise, the only way to spell it correctly is to get totally bladdered and take a run up. By the by, he is the new 14-year-old Karmapa Lama of Tibet. We had spirited him away under the noses of the Chinese Warlords.

It was a very reflective journey for me. During the long periods of silence in the Living Buddha's presence, I chewed on lemon grass and thought much about my own familiar world of business. Here are the reflections:

- America (whatever that is) is still pondering the Microsoft issue – should it, or should it not, be broken up? Of course, the arrival of Dubya's administration, which can clearly be bought, has helped the company defend its own position. If there is one resource that Microsoft has up the wahoo it is greenbacks. The company was charged, if you remember, under anti-trust legislation that is nearly a hundred years old. The legislation was designed to inhibit thugs like Rockefeller, who must be laughing in his grave as Exxon and Mobil, BP and Amoco, most of the banks, the major airlines and nearly all the telecommunications giants are now 're-uniting' with the precise goal of reducing competition. One amusing outcome of the telecoms suicide bombing is that, in the US, the 'Baby Bells', formed by the enforced break-up of the giant Bell Corporation, may be encouraged to re-form to bring some sanity and rationalization to the industry. Hee Hee. The anti-trust legislation predated the concepts of globalism and the need for companies to reinvest BILLIONS of profit in research and development to stay ahead of the game. Did America learn nothing when it completely lost the consumer electronics markets to Japan? I suspect it has already lost leadership in the cell-phone business to Finland (where?), and will shortly lose the exploding e-phone business to – wait for it – Japan. I don't advocate protectionism, but we should not penalize winners for being good and popular. And to win in these kinds of markets you've got to generate more cash for R & D than most of us can get our heads round. I have Windows, and I use the supplied browser. There are other options open to me, all available without getting off my backside. I do not choose to use Microsoft as an ISP. So, WHAT'S THE BIG DEAL? Let 'em get on with it. It's a massive American success – celebrate it.

- There is still a role for anti-trust – and it doesn't always have to be with giants. Andrew Lloyd-Webber recently acquired ten theatres in London's West End, thus securing outlets for his candy-ass pap forever. London is now Europe's most expensive city, and its millions of visitors deserve protection from such institutionalized terrorism.

- Despite lacklustre recent results and a stock price that's a bit gloomy, I like what Uncle Lou (Gersner) did at IBM. *In 1999 they registered 2700 patents, 800 more than anybody else.* That's seed corn for a healthy future. I like the e-trade-only distribution of desktops. I don't recommend stocks, but I wouldn't dump 'em if you've got 'em in the portfolio. When currently delayed IT investments pick up again, they will be in good shape. HP/Compaq might be too wrapped up in internecine stuff to do itself justice – although I remain a fan of Ms Fiorena and was delighted she pulled of the merge against heavy odds.

- Wanna know how Starbucks could add 20% to revenues? Sell appetizing food. Surely it is not beyond the grasp of such (previously) intuitive brand leadership to complement their excellent drinks cabinet with some enticing munchies? So far, four out of ten on this front.

- It's fun to watch Steve Case fall from grace. The combined AOL Time Warner Group has lost the majority of its market value, and the only anti-gravitational forces in there seem to be 'old' technology. Still, when they write the history of this century and/or millennium, let me make a strange prediction – that Case *will be seen as a star*. I believe it will be on the back of what he achieved with AOL before the mega-merge, but that may just be enough. It was that impressive. I think it was Levitt who said: 'The sole purpose of being in business is to create and retain a customer' (and if it wasn't, it should have been). Case is not a techno-freak, and that is *exactly* what he did astonishingly well at AOL. The whole of the e-world has re-learned the age-old lesson – that cool is not the same as profitable. Only a few heeded it on their journey – and

Case never lost sight of it. I hope his journey is not over – but his legacy is secure. He's Legendary with a capital L.

- Steve Jobs has already performed a 'five loaves and five fishes' miracle at Apple. Actually, several times. Er. What's next, Steve? That's going to be the tough one – and if it can be done, he's the guy to do it. But its going to come through the operating system and software, not coloured boxes and (ugh!) specialist (i.e. loss-making) Apple retail stores

- A while ago I forecast the world would develop a fourth cultural and financial epicentre (along with Tokyo, Berlin-London and Washington-New York). It would serve the exploding growth in the *Latino* world. I also forecast that Miami, with everything going for it on the surface, would not become that centre. I hold to that view, unpopular though it may be in south Florida. Every-thing from the airport to the politicians put serious business peo-ple off the place. Add to that the long-running consequences of the farcical 'Elian' mini-series. Then a teaspoon of the Bush/Gore election sitcom, Then add to that its one-eyed parochialism, and you end up with a heady Third-World-type mixture.

- A sign on the bar of the village pub near our English home: *Mo-bilus Phonis Zonus Gratis.* Hallelujah.

- It will be interesting to see in ten years time whether today's mega-mergers actually unlock the shareholder value they're supposed to. The eighties became known as the EWS decade – as billions were invested in Expensive Wrong Solutions in Informa-tion Technology. I suspect many mega-mergers will provide a whole new batch of EWSs.

As I finish my journey with the Living Budda, I am at peace. He is grateful for my raw courage and support throughout this dangerous pilgrimage. Plus the fact I supplied him with an autographed picture of Posh and Becks.

He leaves me with some comforting thoughts: 'It will come to pass, Glasshopper (his little joke), that the rest of your life will be rewarding, and that you will die peacefully in your sleep, smiling, as your grandfather did. You will not die screaming in terror, like his passengers.'

I wonder how he knew about that. Remarkable.

WISDOM FROM
THE LITTLE RED
(BUSINESS) BOOK

You are probably aware that the publishing world is alight. There is frenzied competition for the rights to my next business book. Harry Potter's next efforts are firmly in the shade.

My new work will be a Mao Zedong-style 'Little Red Business Book'. As Bill Gates once articulated his dream that every table should have a PC on it, so my dream is that every working man or woman should have one of these tight little volumes in their pockets. Excepting, of course, on 'Casual Fridays' when the men will have to use some sort of purse.

Bidding for publishing (and movie) rights has reached the high double digits in millions of dollars, euros and pounds. One of the houses involved, bearing in mind the lucrative potential Christian-right-fundamentalist market, has stated that they will remove all expletives from my business maxims. In their case it will be retitled: *A VERY Little Red Business Book*.

Let me give you a tantalizing trailer. One of my wise sayings translates (loosely) as follows: 'Life is as tasty as a crispy-fried duck's foot, then it suddenly kicks you in the groin'. I accept that it loses something when translated from the original Mandarin dialect in which I wrote it, but you get the drift.

I was reminded of it recently. During an average week's research for my writing I read about 700 books, 2500 magazines and spend 5 hours a day on the Web.[1] Somewhere among that lot, I came upon a listing of the Seven 'Modern' Deadly Sins:

- Policies without principles.
- Pleasure without conscience.
- Wealth without work.
- Knowledge without character.
- Industry without morality.
- Science without humanity.
- Worship without sacrifice.

I read it, realized it summed up the complete, unabridged, history of Manchester City, the beloved and minimally blessed soccer team I support, who are (currently) bathed in the light of another false dawn. I then binned it and moved on to the next item.

About an hour later the kick in the groin happened and I found myself scrambling in the trash to find it again. You might want to nip back and reread it before we move on here.

About 5 years ago I finished 25 years in big business, starting as a graduate trainee and ending it as Chairman/CEO of the world's second-biggest branded food chain. The kick in the groin was that, if you took all of the above, jointly and severally, it pretty much described an average day in the last decade of my corporate life. Wind-

1 Although not necessarily in that order.

assisted, I'd knock four of the seven off before lunch. Up to now I hadn't really been sure why I quit. Now I am.

I don't believe I was particularly enlightened *or* particularly Hitlerian. Few business leaders are spectacularly bad or good as *people*, but most of them would squirm a bit if this list were substituted on the office walls for the butt-numbing corporate 'Values' and 'Mission' statements that get stuck up there. It is a LOT nearer reality in most corporations.

The missions and values of most big corporations reflect the dreams, attitudes, character and style of the company's *Grand Fromage*. The personality of the leader – if the leader is worth a damn – is reflected in the corporate persona. It would be inconceivable that it wouldn't be. Now, I know a lot of people used to try and read too much into the 'hidden' values behind my habit of conducting my weekly review meetings with senior executives while I was sat on the lavatory reading *Ulysses*, but they simply missed the subtle reverse irony.

Now, I'll assume you've gone back and reread the 'new' seven sins. Next, you should hold a good-sized paper bag in your right hand and read the following:

> *Our solutions will be bold. We will answer the fundamental needs of the people we live with to ensure harmony, health and prosperity in the world ... Our principles are sacred. We will respect nature and living things, work safely, be gracious to one another and our partners, and each day we will leave for home with consciences clear and spirits soaring.*

Now, throw up in the paper bag you are holding.

The extract is from a corporate mission statement. It happens to be Du Pont (Chemicals), but it doesn't really matter. I have a book of 'em, and there has not been a publication so full of unreadable gobshite since Stephen Hawking's last effort. Not to mention one which includes about 5000 split infinitives ('To better serve.')

Here's a test. You are an average Western CEO: white, male, in your mid-50s with a BUCKETFUL of stock options. There are three weeks to go until you publish the latest earnings figures. You are tracking below analyst's expectations. You need to DO something or the stock price will tank. What creed are you going to follow? Are you going to focus on 'grace' and 'prosperity for the world'? Or are you in for a bit of 'wealth without work'? The latter is also known as fudging the results.

Of the world's top 100 economies, 50 are now corporations. The big companies are getting bigger and they are transcending nations in culture and style. Culture and style include governing missions and values. The people who run them are very similar to those who run the countries. In the main, they are neither very bad nor very good people, but invariably they have been put in place by specific vested-interest groups, and their flexibility and focus will be used to make sure they look after those interests.

This is not new, and it's relatively benign in business. Nobody gets killed. It seems to be creating a lot of wealth. Life goes on. My only wish is that we should be just a wee bit more honest and open about it, and not hide behind self-deluding humbug.

The only danger I see is articulated in my soon-to-be-best-selling *Little Red Business Book*. On the very last page (p. 7) you will find a maxim that translates from the original dialect as follows: 'If, under GAAP, it looks like a duck, quacks like a duck, walks like a duck, and Arthur Andersen says it is a duck, it is a chicken.'

VIVA *EL GATO*

With a start I realize it is more than 47 years since that famous New Year's Eve when Ernesto Guevara and I arrived in Guatemala to begin our apprenticeships as revolutionary guerrillas. He was to become 'Che', of course, to a generation of confused Boomers. To me, however, and a close bunch of his lifetime *companeros*, he would always be 'Ernie'.

Once I had helped him to control his dreadful asthma (with a strict diet of beef tea and lightly-boiled eggs with toast soldiers)[1] he went on to fall under the spell of a bearded fruitcake called Castro. Together they knocked off a revolution in that island just south of

---

1 This diet solved every health problem known to mankind in the north of England in the 1950s. Trust me.

Florida (whose name temporarily escapes me, but whose northern-most suburb is now Miami).

As we moved into the 1960s, the dying Woody Guthrie handed the 'People's Poet' baton to Bob Dylan. At the same time, a sponta-neous photograph of Che ended up, in poster form, on the bedroom walls of millions of student urban-guerrilla wannabes. As Dylan fought with words, Che epitomized the Armed Struggle.

There will, of course, never be another Ernie, just as those times and that *zeitgeist* can never reappear. How could they? Marxism, apart from a couple of places that have lost the plot, is dead. We have wealth creation up the wahoo, low inflation, low interest rates, full employment and have just survived recession that nobody noticed (unless you were one of those picky whiny ones who lost their jobs or their pensions or all their stock options). Sure, there area few holy wars about, and at the time of writing Osama BL has gone under-ground as a waiter in our local Tandoori restaurant. OK, a few Third-World warlords enjoy a bit of genocide now and again, but as far as the Developed West is concerned, we're home dry. There's simply nothing to revolt against.

Or is there?

I have learned never to generalize about Western nations – but my observation is that a lot of responses to the recent anti-capitalist riots moved beyond surprise towards shock. The new overclass sim-ply didn't get it. What the HELL are all these about? Who, or what, is a World Trade Organization? What the hell is a G8 Summit? What in the name of Britney Spears midriff happened at Genoa? How on earth can you get incited to riot about all these?

The answer is that it isn't just the WTO or a G8. These are just magnets attracting a wide range of disillusioned protest. Under-neath it all is the mildly scary fact that our Golden Age is being built on a San Andreas fault. Our society is divided, and this gap is widening.

This time, alienation is not specifically limited to agricultural workers, or craftsmen, or factory workers, or administrative staff as it has been in the past. It is affecting the whole mid-range of society – the working family. The massive rewards of our Golden Age are being siphoned off to a tiny percentage of the population, and the benefits are being spread very thinly elsewhere. Many are going backwards.

Full employment is a myth by conventional definitions. Sure there are jobs – but the growth areas are in outsourced services and pizza delivery, where minimum wage proliferates, and benefits and security are nonexistent. In London, it costs six pounds an hour to park your car at a meter. If you work in the city at a fast food joint on minimum wage, you can look out of the window and see an *iron pole earning more than you do.* In England we have actually found a creative way to redistribute wealth UPWARDS (i.e. from poor to rich) via a privately run lottery.

In the US, a recent survey shows that the richest 20% of the population have increased their wealth substantially over the last decade – while the poorest 20% have remained static. In New York, the latter have actually become poorer. Also in the US, minorities leaving high school will now do so with the same grade average as whites, but they will start their adult life with only 10% of the average family net worth of their white counterparts.

In South Africa, outside the cultured lawns of Capetown, two million 'blacks' and 'coloureds' live in the townships. I have seen them, and I do not believe the status quo is sustainable. I have also seen soup kitchens in Washington DC, within a Tiger Woods' three-iron distance of the White House.

Our Golden Age hasn't changed the fact there are still too many poor people in rich countries, and too many rich people in poor ones. A gap is appearing – and widening – between the really REALLY rich and everybody else. A similar gap occurred in France in the late eighteenth century. Look what happened there

The words of Ernie echo around my brain. Clearly, it is both my heritage and fate to lead the new revolution. The world needs a new Robespierre. I may look an unlikely revolutionary guerrilla, being a middle-aged Englishman currently sporting more chins that the Beijing Telephone Directory, but one simply has to answer this sort of call. From now on, I will answer only to the name of *El Gato* (website: *www.ElGato.com)*. My first target will be to take out the international headquarters of the filthy capitalist IMF. That's if somebody can tell me where it is. At this stage I am not contemplating the use of a suicide bomb strategy, as there is only one of me and that might be counterproductive to my long-term goals, but I rule nothing out in the future.

We will need money, of course. For me to purge this capitalist icon, I will need several heat-seeking missiles, at least one bazooka, a small tank (preferably four-wheel-drive), some sandwiches and one of those, you know, ski-mask things. Unfortunately Mother Russia is currently between cheque books, so I will have to ask you, Mr & Mrs Joe and Josephine Public, to stump up. For your convenience, I am suggesting an individual contribution of £10,000. Also for your convenience, I suggest your cheque is made payable to 'Cash' – or you can wire it direct to the Revolutionary Bank Of Switzerland, ref: *ElGato2094451B.*

You must now eat this book, otherwise I will have to kill you.

THE RETURN OF *EL GATO*

Christianstaad, St Croix: Our revolution explodes into life. I am, as you know, and assuming you had the manners to read the last chapter, now named *El Gato*.

My mission is first to overthrow capitalism, and then restructure it in such a way that the mid-range demographic (teachers, engineers, home-makers, small-business owners, business journalists etc.) gets more of a share of the humungous national wealth being created. Our credo is summarized by an unknown US labour specialist from (yes!) Berkeley, who boasts the unlikely name of Harley Shaiken. He calls us the 'Proletariat of the Information Age'.

Here in St Croix, in our maximum security headquarters in a corner of the bar at the Buccaneer Hotel, I link up with the White-

Collar Rasta Movement (motto: *We be hummin'*). Our plans, covert for so long, are being triggered with devastating effect:

- First, we will activate one of our longest dormant 'moles', buried deeply inside the US Establishment – namely Alan Greenspan. We last brought him into play just after the turn of the millennium, when, with a few well chosen public words, he wiped more than ten percent off the value of the Dow and trampled NASDAQ into the shredding bin. All in one day. This sort of thing, of course, only damages the targeted few. The time has now come for the real meltdown.
- Next, we move on to Boeing. Our movement has already united the 19,000-strong Society of Professional Engineering Employees in an almost unprecedented way. Their sole previous collective action was a one-day walk out in 1992. Now they are united, with devastating strikes a part of everyday life. We also bring into play our mole in the design department, and cleverly jeopardize the company's future by getting them to fight the upcoming competition from Europe's Airbus with the wrong-sized plane at the wrong time. Enough? You would think so, but not for us. Their whole accounting integrity is now under threat after the work of another of our moles is uncovered – with unsubstantiated operating profits obviously running back through the years. Irrevocable damage has already been done – both to the company and capitalism.
- Our activists in Gillette surface. This once mighty company suffers from the (relative) failure of their new MACH3 razor, which is due primarily to a massive covert campaign by our (male) members to buy the new product. However – and this is brilliant – they then TREBLE the number of times they use the blade compared to the old one before throwing it away. This magnificent strategy brings Gillette to its knees.
- One single agent in Proctor & Gamble telephones the analysts with an early millennium earnings warning – which wipes $37

billion of the market value of the company and drags the Dow down 350 points – all this in ONE DAY. High fives and more rum punch!!!! Many more are planned – some before you read this.

- Enron? It was just too easy. Scary, really.
- 'Elian' – the code name for our agent in the French government (and I use the word 'government' in its loosest possible sense) – activates one of our international cells. He calls in a few chips and forces through legislation that signals a mandatory 35 hour week for all but the smallest French businesses. Within days, the French truckers, many of them independent businesses, understandably unhappy at being told that their massive investments in trucks can only work for 35 out of 168 hours available each week, strike and bring the country to a halt.
- In Germany, of course, I personally delivered a package of private papers to the newspapers. They held secrets that until now I have kept to myself. But no more. Within hours, Helmut Kohl, until recently the Chancellor-Father figure of modern (united) Germany, is disgraced and the Christian Democrat Party brought to its knees.
- The head of BAB,[1] our flourishing female organization, was recently appointed (and then more recently departed) as CEO of Mattel after having completed her project – to destroy the company. This is a simple but devastating strategy: we put a mole in place who, over a period of a couple of years, takes every incorrect strategic option available, and then leaves. It also seems to be working in Kmart and British Airways. Clearly, the latter should have kept Go, the cut-price airline, and sold the fancy, expensive, flatbed, unprofitable stuff. This kind of damage (by us) can take decades to recover.
- Finally, we put into place our grandest gameplan. To achieve our goals we MUST effectively control the engine room of the last great Super-Power, the Presidency of the US. Just as in 1996, we

---

1 Breasts Against the Bourgeoisie.

used Chinese funds to make sure our preferred candidate got the job. This time, by expensively rigging the election in Florida, we got our man in. Our plan is this: Dubya hands out trillions of dollars in tax cuts, based on projected surpluses that *we will make sure never materialize*. Doom, debt and gloom will occur, in reverse order. He will also have to pay back all those 'investors' who paid cash to get him into office, and we will see a programme of myopic protectionism begin – particularly in steel and agriculture. This will, of course, bring retaliation, and capitalism will glurp down the planet's plughole while the intercontinental missiles of a global trade war whiz overhead. When I look at Bush, and think what is ahead, it is hard not to think of the words of Oscar Wilde on the death of Little Nell. You would have to have a heart of stone not to laugh.

With that thought I will leave you. As *El Gato*, I must go underground again. Maybe for months.

ZERO TOLERANCE? MAKE MY DAY ...

There is a misconception that 'Zero Tolerance' is new. It isn't. I was present when it was invented in its post-Attila form. It was 1974, and the location was a soccer field, south of London. We were playing a side with a notoriously nasty guy in their attack, and I was one of our two central defenders charged with damage constraint. We failed. After about ten minutes, he broke through the pair of us, and, as the ball ran through to our goalkeeper, this Monster followed through and smashed his studs (a.k.a. cleats in the US) into the face of our man.

There were teeth everywhere on the grass. As I arrived, the victim, a close friend who shared an apartment with a bunch of us, greeted me by putting his tongue out through the new hole in his cheek. As I looked for a quiet spot to throw up, my co-defender arrived on the scene.

These were the days when a good amateur soccer player anywhere in the UK, who worked for a big company, would find himself transferred down to the London headquarters of the company to play for the Company Team – even if he couldn't add up and scratched his arse a lot. This guy had arrived from Dundee, in Scotland, on such a mission, although, in fairness, I never saw him scratch his arse. His maths were also good enough for him to work out when he was due to buy a round of drinks, and to then exit in pursuit of a suddenly remembered urgent phone call. When he arrived at the scene of the crime, however – which was, by now, looking like an out-take from M.A.S.H. – it was as though he had been living for this day. Zero Tolerance was invented right there and then.

It took us 40 more minutes to get our revenge. I confess the only part I played in it was, at a given signal that had been pre-agreed by the pair of us, when the referee was not looking, I stood on our target's toes and grabbed his shirt. He was thus immobilized for a second or two. During that time my buddy committed the most appalling foul that I have ever witnessed on this guy. Hannibal Lecter would have disowned him. I simply won't describe it, and I shudder at its memory. But it was a thing of great beauty, and perfection, in its own field of specialty.

From these humble roots, Zero Tolerance abounds today. Kids are being tried as adults for serious crimes. 'Three Strikes and you're OUT' is – unbelievably – now an accepted legal doctrine in the US. In Texas, they have outdoor executions on the first sunny days of spring. The world marvels at what was achieved with New York's crime figures under the Fiefdom of Mayor Giuliani. There are prices to pay, of course, but as long as the collateral damage is not TOO sickening, the aggregate seems worth it. All of which confirms one of my long-held beliefs – which is that a population does not get the governance it wants, it gets what it deserves.

What of Zero Tolerance in the exciting world of modern business? Er ... well ... not much, really.

I am resolute in my belief that business crime abounds in the form of, for example, insider trading. Statutes like GAAP are a laugh. Regulation remains weak where powerful lobbyists pay for it to be so, and cloyingly nannyish where they don't or can't. Tolerance is nowhere near zero here. Abuses of power abound daily on Planet Business, and some lives are hell as a result. Most of them are tolerated.

What of the tolerance level for good ole continued poor performance? It sometimes defies belief. A few years ago, for reasons known only to themselves, the board of British Airways appointed an in-house lawyer, Bob Ayling, as CEO. I've nothing against lawyers as you know, my observation being that it's only 99% of them that give the rest a bad name. But this guy was a fathead from the get-go. Confrontational with all the wrong people and blessed with Saddam Hussein's eye for a PR own-goal, this meatloaf oversaw the semi-demise of a genuinely great airline – one which HAD strong profitability and a good reputation. Incredibly, he was tolerated for four years before he was punted.

Here, of course (and you can pick 50 examples of your own from blue chip companies all over the developed world), high-tolerance is almost built in. A board who appoint a CEO don't want to face up to the fact TOO QUICKLY that they have appointed a plonker. In some cases, a reverse set of tolerance guarantees come into play – the CEO has APPOINTED the board who oversee his/her performance. It's hardly a formula for Zero Tolerance – and don't expect it to change quickly.

There is an area where I would LOVE to see Zero Tolerance come into business. The whole ethos and approach to corporate bankruptcy now stinks. It is an epidemic in the US, and it is a trend I forecast will creep over the Atlantic. Companies are now seeking Chapter 11 or hopping in to administration when they are solvent and cash positive. It is increasingly seen as a viable manoeuvre to avoid litigation or liability. Frequently, it is not the creditors who force the issue, but the company itself declares it, rather like stepping into a shelter when you see rain cloud coming over. It is WAY, WAY too easy to spit on the interests of stockholders and/or creditors, and use bankruptcy to mask the results of bad management or as a way of easing some merger through.

There was once a stigma attached to being bankrupt. In Europe (Germany in particular) it was all but a criminal offence to become bankrupt. It was, *as it should be*, a LAST DESPERATE resort, not a day-to-day tactic.

My co-defender in that famous soccer 1974 match, alas, is no longer on this earth. I often raise a metaphoric glass to his memory. I am making him this promise. I have a few investments left. Should any of those companies, that have the privilege of my investment, declare bankruptcy in a way that does not RESPECT my interests, they will find me one day hiding by the executive elevator. I will be wearing my old football boots. When the CEO emerges, I will spring, and stand on his or her toes and grab his or her shirt. I will then summon up the spirit of my departed friend, and attempt the famous foul. Whether I will achieve the same effect is doubtful. But Zero Tolerance will have arrived in business. On that you can rely.

AN APPLE A DAY ...

History fascinates me. For nearly 30 years I have had Jacob Bronowski's glorious essays on the *Ascent Of Man* (Little, Brown and Co. 1974) close to my beside. I love his description of the Pythagorean fortress-palace at Alhambra, the last monument of Arab civilization in Europe. Go back to the fifteenth century, and share his vision of what went on inside the *Sala de las Camas*, its most sacred chamber:

> *Here, the girls from the harem came from the bath and reclined, naked. Blind musicians played in the gallery and the eunuchs padded about. The Sultan watched from above, and sent an apple down to signal the girl of his choice ...*

I introduced the 'Apple Game' into Burger King's world head-quarters when I began my spell as Chairman and CEO in the early 1990s. It was a tremendous success for a few days, until the head of HR informed me that it was breaking (approximately) 17,611 local, state and federal employment laws – as well as violating as many as 30,000 constitutional civil rights and most of the ADA.

I know pens will leap into many hands now – and accuse me of supporting hedonism, slavery, chauvinism and so on. OK, I'll take the hit – but all I'm saying is that these folk knew how to throw a party.

A more serious point is that we in business should be inspired by history. Buried in various places in it are all the lessons we could ever need – even in the most modern, high-technology environments. It should, therefore, be a major concern for all of us that the quality and content of history teaching in schools today is appalling. In both the UK and US, the sins of omission are frequently added to by misrepresentation. In England, we are taught that Dunkirk was a brilliant victory. In the US, the (approximately) seventy million questions any high school pupil with half a brain would naturally ask about the rise of the white man are never answered. Simply because they are never asked.

Despite the worrying educational trends of dumbing down and lying, history is there for all of us. But that's only if we bother to look. If there were no business schools or gurus, just think of the great lessons history has for modern business. Here are four for a start:

- Great goals can be achieved by aggression or luck. But sometimes they are achieved by *sheer dogged perseverance* against overwhelming odds. The great journeys (Lewis and Clark, Antarctica); the great mountain conquests (Everest); the great voyages (Columbus, Heyerdahl); the great technical breakthroughs (measuring longitude) – all these were achieved by good old bloody-minded resilience. By just refusing to be beaten. That is a mantra that many entrepreneurs, with their vulnerable start-up companies and low levels of capital and credit – but with their glorious dreams – will recognize as relevant and modern.

- Contests happen and competition exists. So do victories and victors. In the main it is healthy – or so Darwin convinced us. But what history has also shown us many times is that *mindless oppression by victors does not create a sustainable solution*. The seeds of the horrendous World War II were sewn in the myopic demands of the victors of World War I. The Chinese have a saying that a deal is worthless unless BOTH parties can leave the table with something to smile about. In the world of mega-mergers and acquisitions this lesson should be crayoned on the wall of every boardroom.

- We have learned that whatever political, religious or social 'superstructure' you force over the heritage of the people involved – *it can take a long time for the existing cultures to erode*. The 'creation' of Yugoslavia forced an oppressive statehood over the centuries-old religious chasms of the Balkans. At the first opportunity – i.e. the removal of the oppressor – those cultures and that heritage proved that they were still alive. The lines drawn on a map at the end of the 1940s, supposedly creating Pakistan and India, simply added more fuel to the fire of a centuries-old tension. It's still there, by the way. What a lesson there for an American company hoping to do business in China. Or a UK company acquiring an Italian subsidiary. Or a brash modern company taking over a conservative old firm.

- We have also learned that *no one race has a monopoly of wisdom OR idiocy* (with the exception of the Irish who, on occasion, appear to have both). The English-speaking peoples (as Churchill called them) have produced great literature, architecture and scientific breakthroughs. They also invented slavery and concentration camps. The African nations have produced great statesmen, and genocidal war lords as a by-product. China's history is a paradox of graceful learning and disgraceful oppression. The lesson for business is clear – no race, creed, gender, age group, department, region or function has a monopoly of what you need for business success. They, however, all contribute. *But they are ALL capable of own goals.* Make sure you have the positives of diversity, but be aware of the dangers.

Studying history can also help you answer those day-to-day questions that niggle you when you can't come up with an answer, such as: *'Why is there a Scotland?'* Well, believe it or not, it has a role to play. History shows us that Scotland provides the only nation on this planet where the family and given names of all its males are *completely interchangeable.* Example: 'Have you see Cameron Fraser?' 'Yes, he's over there, standing by Fraser Cameron'. 'Thanks. My name's Murdoch Douglas, by the way'. 'How nice to meet you. I'm Douglas Murdoch'

In this, they stand alone.

HAVE IT YOUR WAY ...

It is one of the more entertaining themes of American history that Burger King has a mid-life crisis every ten years or so. Ten years ago, one was raging. In hindsight I'm not sure I was part of the solution, or the problem. I think I may have been both.

Noting the current one, as it takes down the *For Sale* sign and ponders its new future under the parentage of Texas Pacific Group, I can reveal my own near-miss when it comes to ownership of this great old battleship of a brand. Representatives from a group of Chinese gangs approached me some time ago to lead a buyout of this famous American icon-brand. They offered me very attractive personal terms – a base salary of $2 billion a year (paid offshore), stock options that would be worth double-digit billions of dollars over three years (against some very conservative stock price goals, with the built-in ability to restate the option price if things go wrong), two private jets, Jennifer Lopez as my personal 'Executive Assistant' and six free Whopper coupons each and every week. It is with some reluctance I turned them down. One must never go back.

I was, of course, plagued by the media for my commentary on what is going on. Franchisees were splashing about in the water and trying to 'buy' the system. Lawsuits and counter-suits were all over the radar screen. Again I refused to comment specifically – I have never been inside the door since I left and have no idea what is going on. But on the subject of franchising systems generally, I am happy to share my monopoly of wisdom. I hide it beneath my scar tissue.

There are two basic laws that govern franchising of a branded quick-service restaurant (QSR) retail system. The first concerns the quality of operations. In a system of any significant size, there will be a wide range of quality of such operations. In the US, this is called the Subway Rule. When there are both franchised and company-owned operations, another rule comes into force. It is that the franchisees will occupy the positions at *both* ends of the quality spectrum. The best franchisees are brilliant. When they are just very good, there is no doubt that an enlightened and capable franchisee will run a better operation than the company. But when they are bad, they are truly gruesome.

It is embarrassing to the franchisor, but company operations usually score a bit above halfway on the scale. They score what Tom Peters, in a moment of unrecorded inspiration with me prior to going on stage at a Burger King conference, once memorably called Ho Fucking Hum grades. Or HFH as we subsequently called it. Quite. I haven't heard anybody, before or since, describe the condition in a better way.

The second natural law concerns the ownership – and 'management' – of the brand. Ownership in a franchised, branded, retail system can be confusing. If you add up the 'branded' assets owned by the individual franchisees (i.e. the bricks and mortar, real estate and so on), it will probably exceed the total of branded assets owned by the company which actually *owns and manages the brand* (the franchisor). It does not seem a big intellectual step to then say that it would make sense for the franchisees to own the brand itself, and control their own destiny.

Dead wrong.

I have seen things on *Star Trek* that are more credible than the output of a routine franchisee meeting. Franchisees are the LAST people on earth who should own their own system.

Most of these retail markets are ultra-competitive today, and that means a brand has to stay restless. It needs constant refreshment and reinvention. There is a need to keep investing. Sometimes you have to spend just to defend – in response to competitive initiatives. You have to contemplate risky and untried stuff. You often have to move fast.

Franchisees are a strongly bonded community. There is powerful peer group chemistry. There is a lot of sympathy for the guy in the group who is having a hard time, or who hasn't the resources to invest in anything risky. When a range of options are identified, if the franchisees are left to choose one they will naturally polarize to the one which is easiest for the least-well-off of their community. They become shallow-end paddlers. That's a terminal illness for a modern brand.

The ownership – and management – of a franchised brand has to be in the hands of somebody detached from those pressures. It needs to be in the hands of what Machiavelli called an 'armed prophet' – somebody who will kick the system (if necessary) into taking the necessary uncomfortable and risky decisions, and to move away from the lowest common denominator.

It doesn't make for a comfortable life for the franchisor. With the changing face of capital markets and (seemingly) eternally low interest rates, and the growing habit of seeking a legal remedy for every tin-pot dispute, I suspect that we have seen the end of the explosive growth of franchised systems. If the late, great Jim McLamore was starting Burger King today, I doubt he would choose franchising for growth. It is interesting to note that Howard Schultz largely avoided it for Starbucks.

Which leads me to the third and final law governing franchising. It is Gibbons' Universal rule on the subject:

> *If there is peace, tranquillity and a lot of smiling between franchisee and franchisor, the system is REALLY sick. Probably terminally. It just doesn't know it yet.*

Hang on. Did they say Jennifer *Lopez*? Where's that bit of paper ...

YES, WE HAVE NO BANANAS

Inspired by America's leading politicians (and who wouldn't be) I recently held a series of sold-out 'town hall' meetings across the land. I plan to introduce this way of working to England, and have already booked a series of dates with Prince Charles, Tony Benn and Bob Geldof. This is how I keep in touch with the Great Unwashed (i.e. those who do not work for 'New Economy' companies and other such underclasses).

At the end of these meetings, I usually take a few questions before I am whisked away in my limo to the late-night television chat shows that invariably inhibit my quest for evenings of mild hedonism. When I get there, one of the most frequently questions asked is: 'Barry – what exactly is a Corporate Culture, and how would I recognize one if it bit me in the groin?'

Rather like many such legends before me, I do not like to give a straight answer. I speak in fables. Here's one that hides the answer:

Put five apes in a cage. Hang a banana from the ceiling, and put some stairs right underneath it.

When the first ape starts to climb the stairs (as one will) spray all the apes with cold water. When another ape starts to climb the stairs, spray them all again.

If, later, another ape tries to climb the stairs, the others will prevent him. Even though there is no water spray.[1]

Now, replace one ape with a new one. The new ape sees the banana, but when he goes to get it he is attacked by the others.

Repeat this by replacing another of the original apes with another new one. The newest will also go for the banana, and will also be attacked. The first newcomer will join in the attack with enthusiasm.

Repeat again. This time the newcomer is again attacked – by a group that includes two newcomers who have no idea why they are attacking the new guy.

After the fourth and fifth original apes are similarly re- placed, all the ones originally sprayed with cold water are gone. But no ape approaches the stairs or the banana. Why not?

Because 'That's the way it's always been around here.'

There are two reasons why that piece caught my eye. First, the apes are male – although I'm sure they don't have to be to make the point. However, with the experience of 30 years in business in both the US and UK, in my observation, the authors were right to do that. There are days when the business-male of the species rates between Nean- derthal and Dickhead on the brightness scale.

---

1 Unless they support the Manchester United soccer team.

The second reason it struck a chord with me was that it described EXACTLY the disease Burger King suffered around the start of the nineties. The symptoms varied, but that was the malady.

Now, read it again, and ponder. You will see it hides much more. It is at the core of this 'corporate culture' thing and leads us to a simple definition of the concept – that a corporate culture is how people in an organization *THINK and BEHAVE for better or for worse*. What's more, it is how they do these when no-one is looking. It is not how the 'Corporate Values Statement', which is pinned so imperiously on so many cafeteria walls, says they SHOULD think and behave. Nor is it how the CEO thinks they OUGHT to. And it is not just about the thoughts and behaviours of a few people, but those of any and all of them.

What the apes also show us is how this thing goes wrong. Through no great malice or wrongdoing, a set of thoughts and behaviours that were relevant in the past still exist when the times, circumstances and people which all shaped them have long gone.

Is it really important? Or is it just a nice-to-have? If you dig deeply into the causes of IBM hitting its iceberg around the start of the 1990s, the behaviour of the IBM-apes[2] was fundamental. And it had been so for a long time. The company had atrophied. I believe IBM eventually lost around $75 billion in market value before it recovered. Yes, I did say $75 billion, and this was more than decade ago when a billion was still a lot of money. It can be that devastating.

There is no one-size-fits-all for corporate culture. But it is the END result of causes, not a cause of an end result. You can't write the rules of corporate culture down, or provide an operating manual. Those are both wholly self-defeating exercises. Wall Street's comedic rush around the turn of the millennium to let people wear casual clothes and male earrings in an attempt to stop the brain drain to the different culture of dotcoms was just that – a joke. A culture does

2 This is the same IBM which was lead by Thomas Watson in 1943. That's the same Thomas Watson that opined that there would be a world market for about *five* computers. Things eventually changed in the 1990s.

not result in clothes. Clothes make a culture. The former approach is So Sad.

The key to it is to create healthy air in the corporate greenhouse – and then stand back and let the people's thoughts and behaviour shape your culture for you. It can be done. I am no great fan of any of the current Captains of Industry, but I preceded Howard Schultz (of Starbucks) on a business convention platform recently. I'm normally out of these places like a rat up a drainpipe when I'm done, but I was still taking my microphone off when he started, and caught his opening words. I was hooked after the first moments. Here is a mighty modern brand, and here is the man who built it – still underpinning everything he does with a genuine respect for the human spirit. And I am not, for once, bullshitting. I was *there*. He believes the resultant 'culture' is THE key market differentiator for Starbucks. So do I. It is now a huge company, with thousands of outlets, and it gets harder and harder. He may yet lose it – but ten out of ten for understanding what needed to be done and for *trying*.

So take a deep breath – and go right up to those steps in your own corporate cage, climb them, take the banana and eat it. It is unlikely you will be hosed. And if you do this wearing no clothes, and on your backside you have painted, in lime green, the words 'Please take your compromise outside and suck it', I guarantee your corporate culture will change. In something less than a heartbeat.

WHAT NEWS FROM THE RIALTO?

Where to go in spring is such a problem. None of my old haunts is attractive just now – even Miami, Havana's northernmost suburb. I am driven to distraction by the gurgling sound made by things as they swirl round just before they go down the plughole. In this case they are being emitted by the national ambitions of at least one of the gaggle of local mayors. How some of these guys beat the other ten billion sperm to get here in the first place is beyond me.

London threatens to sink under the weight of the Queen's Jubilee. With the hoo-ha surrounding the recent deaths of the Queen 'A Lifetime of Service' Mother, and Princess 'A Lifetime of Service' Margaret, adding to the sheer tension of waiting for Charles to be allowed to goose Camilla in public, it is becoming too much. I need to get out.

I go to New York, but there is no peace. As I chew on a dish of minuscule Bay of Biscay *elba* in *Il Buco,* the Big Apple's new dining hot spot for We Who Know Such Places, my serenity is disturbed by the shrill cries of the living dead. These, of course, are the now zombie-like recent dotcom billionaires who have seen their paper fortunes ravaged (and in some cases defenestrated) by Wall Street's recent scorched earth policy towards their stocks.

There is no alternative. I travel to Venice. On the surface, I do this at the request of a small but powerful sub-committee of the International Monetary Fund. The plan is for me to give a signal of public support for the beleaguered €uro. By spreading around some strategic purchases of *grappa* and *gelato* it is felt I can lead it back to parity with the US greenback.[1]

While I am doing the normal 'tourist' things – kicking fat pigeons in Piazza San Marco (my record distance is 12.5 metres, although with a slight wind behind), and sipping espresso while pretending not to notice the, shall we say, aggressive public courting habits of the local young couples – my mind moves on to deeper things.

Venice is a thought-provoking location to try and come to grips with what is going on in the high-speed world of modern capitalism. It was here, centuries ago, around the Rialto, that the idea of making huge amounts of money, just for the sake of it, was really born. I must say it was an idea that caught on, and gathered momentum.

The Venetians treated the Crusades rather like a seedy Caribbean port treats a visiting cruise liner full of tourists from Wisconsin – each of them weighing 350 lb and wearing tight spandex shorts. The Crusades, in terms of the financial opportunity offered to people interested in this new idea of getting rich, were like the dotcoms of the day. The Venetians cleverly sided with *neither* cause. They sold T-shirts that boldly supported Richard *Coeur de Lion*, while others proclaimed '*Infidels Suck*'. They made humongous amounts of money from both sides.

---

1 This takes me about two months to achieve.

As I stare into the bottle green waters of the Grand Canal, I begin to see where it all started to go wrong.

The idea of 'limited liability' is often cited as the great catalyst of modern capitalism. By limiting an investor's potential loss to the amount invested, two things happened. First, it opened up vast potential 'external' investment funds to ravenously hungry businesses. Second, it enabled the ownership of a business – or a share of the ownership of a business – to be detached from running it. Without these two factors, the explosive growth of the last two to three centuries would never have happened.

These two growth hormones are now, however, playing a part in the bad news – the volatility and mood swings of today's investment markets. It can be argued that there is now *too much* external money available for limited liability investment. The money supply in the Western economies is too loose. Boomers have got discretionary funds coming out of every bodily orifice. Retained corporate earnings are strong, with companies often using them to buy back their own stocks and further restrict supply of shares in the market. Institutional investors roam the streets looking for good homes for their trillions. Interest rates are heading towards negative territory.

The surplus money supply position will also get worse as Boomers receive inheritances on an unprecedented scale, politicians seek tax cuts to offset projected budget 'surpluses' and technology keeps boosting productivity and earnings. Even with the dotcom bubble burst, Osama BL having done his party trick, and the major stock markets repositioned downwards, stock prices are still at a level beyond anything that can be justified by a sane multiple of sustainable earnings. The only price justification is still that if I buy it at X, I think I will be able to sell it at X plus. Somewhere, somehow.

The detachment of ownership from involvement has also now reached fantasy levels – particularly as technology moves a lot of big modern businesses far beyond the understanding of many investors. It was easy to understand a railway or a cotton mill. Although an investor would not have necessarily understood how electricity worked, it was easy to see what it could do. But does anybody really know what the wonderful Cisco actually *does*? If I gave you a crayon, could you draw a Sun Microsystem? Does anybody, other than a handful of clued-up folk, understand where the information age is leading – and why one stock is a 'must-have' and another is doomed?

We have all this available money chasing businesses we don't understand, now coupled with 24-hour, 12-time-zone, e-trading. We also have a sensory overload of 'information' on any and every hourly corporate development everywhere. Is it any surprise we have overheating and violent part-market mood swings? It will get worse.

Could unlimited liability, in some form, make a comeback? *Should* it – if only to bring sanity back to investing? The answer must be no. The only place it has been institutionalized in modern business was in the Lloyds of London syndicates, and the downside when it went wrong was horrendous. Plus the noise of the victims squealing like stuck pigs was nauseating.

If sanity does reappear it will be through the normal route of self-correction and vested self-interest. But this one will be a white-water ride, and there's no sign of calm and control yet.

Which reminds me. I have this dotcom start-up that could be huge. No, honestly. It's called MiamiClassActs.com. We are short of content at the moment, but that will change. We expect to think of at least one act before the year end. We just need a couple of billion dollars – nothing much really – for marketing. You know the kind of thing: a handful of two-minute spots at half-time on the Super Bowl. Our burn rate is tightness itself – with central overheads pinned down to $67 million a month. We conservatively expect revenues to soar past the $10-a-week mark within three years, and hope to reverse the current trend on narrowing margins soon.

E-mail me and I'll send you a prospectus.

JURY'S STILL OUT

After the last *debacle* I have taken on responsibility for the quality control of the new millennium.

My first report is encouraging. As we noted earlier, the feared Y2K bug, considered by some a shoo-in to wipe out the earth's IT systems, didn't happen. What did arrive, of course, was the first widespread computer virus. The one that made the breakthrough, and a lot of money for Norton anti-virus software, was called the *I Love You* bug. This happily wiped out much of the world's e-mail.

It turned out to have been instigated by a young, inarticulate, spotty, code-writing oik in the Philippines. Possibly helped by his girlfriend, who would be, using my definition, an oikess. We filed all this information twice – once under 'Scary' and once under 'Comical'.

Nevertheless, the millennium moves on. As ever, the business environment is changing – but sometimes in ways even the gurus couldn't foresee.

The first event of significance for business that I have to report on is the death of the jury system. This was invented, in England, in the year 1179 – the same year as the non-stick codpiece.[1] It has, therefore, lasted an honourable 821 years. Some of us mourn its passing.

The writing has been on the wall for a while. O.J. Simpson showed that, if you spend $8 million, you can get a jury to put the telescope to their blind eyes when looking at DNA evidence. The distinguished fat bastard called Robert Maxwell (among others) showed that much of modern corporate business is so complex that it can become impossible to isolate and identify a tort. The jury system took these batterings, but still it hung on with flickering vital signs. It took the good old US judicial system generally, and my beloved south Florida's system specifically, to issue the *coup de grace.*

To get the millennium off to a flyer, a Miami jury awarded the estate of a murdered Dutch tourist several million dollars. The murder took place in a tough area of Miami, into which the tourist had strayed by mistake. The award went against – wait for it – the company who rented the tourist a car. This rental took place 250 miles away from Miami, halfway up the other coast of Florida. The car rental company obeyed every law associated with car renting – that is not disputed. But it did not warn the tourist that, should he drive the 250 miles to Miami, he should not go in certain murder-friendly areas.

The powerful voice of this writer shouts in sympathy with the family of the deceased. But this voice does not stop there. This voice, known throughout the civilized world as a voice of controlled, calm conservatism, rises, Roy Orbison-like, a full three octaves, to denounce that jury, collectively and individually, as Dickheads.

---

1 Rumour has it that an early version of GAP, the clothing retailer, rushed to market a 'Relaxed Fit' version of the codpiece. It was a best-seller.

Incidentally, one outcome of this – and you can file this under 'Only in America' or 'I'm not making this up' – emerged when I rented a car in Miami just weeks ago. I had lived there for twelve years prior to returning to the UK permanently – and was revisiting the place a year or so after I had left. Some things had already changed, but I did not feel the need for a map to accompany my car – as I know the place like the back of my hand. When I declined the map (are you ready for this?) I had to sign a *legal release indicating I had declined the offer of a map and accepting all possible direct and indirect consequences thereof.*

During my next weekly phone review sessions with Mr Bush and Lionel Blair, I shall be advising them to abandon the jury system for good. Like the position of the Mayor of London, it serves no useful purpose.

Barely have we digested the implications of this blow, but the new millennium puts a toe-tag on the second big corpse of the New Age. I refer, of course, to democracy.

Not many of you will know this, but George Dubya Bush spent the early months of the new millennium desperately trying to convince me to join his ticket as his vice presidential candidate. Stupid man. First of all, the US Constitution has a fairly clear position on the possibilities of a foreign-born candidate (summarized here as 'No'). That wasn't a good enough reason for G.W., however, and it was only after a four-hour concentrated discussion that I managed to convince him that I wasn't an African-American woman.

It is one of my late life pleasures to see thousands, nay millions, of bright young people joining me in my lifelong campaign to end voting. I prophesy that the next US presidential and UK parliamentary elections will record the lowest ever turnout. My plan is working.

My plan is to defend democracy, as it is dying like the coral reefs. Our fathers didn't fight for me to vote for somebody who makes me up-chuck. They didn't go to war so that some US guy could spend nearly $70 million of vested-interest money to win the presidential *primaries*. They didn't die for elections that are play-offs between

Big Business, the tobacco industry, fancy-Dan lobbyists, mad-hatter religious fundamentalists, gun-freaks, and organized labour.[2]

It doesn't matter who wins an election today in almost any of the big 'democracies'. Power lies in the ability to make the decisions that follow. That power is now out of the reach of, and cannot be[1] influenced by, the ordinary voter. *That position is mirrored exactly in big corporations*, and in its implications for the ordinary shareholder or employee.

Democracy will have to die first, but here's my plan to get it back. We all stop voting. Within 25 years national elections in the US and UK will be won by tennis scores (i.e. 6–3, 4–6, 6–2). Now, one thing that politicians can't stand is being *ignored*. So, we will get back to democracy via industrial-strength apathy. In the meantime, families, communities and businesses (particularly small ones) will have to take on additional responsibilities – education, health care, justice, blah blah blah. But, when we do that, all of those will be BETTER and CHEAPER. And when 'they' come back, we will only let them get involved on our terms – that the cost of government must be less than one twelfth of the nation's annually produced wealth. It's foolproof.

Certainly, it seems a depressing start to the New Age – with both the jury system and democracy lying cold on the slab. But all is not lost. We are still being entertained. Plans have been announced by the National Rifle Association, lead by (honestly) Charlton Heston,[3] for an NRA *themed restaurant*.

I was 54 years old at the start of the millennium, 56 as I write this. I don't know how much I will see of it. But if I were to live right through it, I would not come across a dafter idea or a bigger pillock proposing it.

---

2 And that's just Florida …
3 I understand the UK branch may be led by Millwall Football Club.

BILL AND ME –
SUCH GOOD LOSERS

A while ago, I went to Las Vegas to give a speech to some deserving business people. The Eiffel Tower outside my hotel was, I believe, only slightly bigger than the original. Quickly, I entered into the spirit of the place and sat in front of an automated poker machine. Seconds later, I headed off to my room, depressed and $40 poorer. I turned on CNN, and heard that Bill Gates' diary for the same day would record that he had also 'lost' some money on that day. In his case it was $9 billion, as the value of his stake in Microsoft tumbled. I know exactly how he felt.

At the time, the stock price of Microsoft was discounting America's worst-kept secret – that a US District Court Judge called Thomas Penfield Jackson, a man miraculously named after the whole of Manchester City's reserve team midfield early in the 1933/4 season, would punish the company for its crimes against humanity by demanding they write 50 lines, stand in the corner of the classroom and break up into two or three bits. Each of them bigger than Canada, and certainly of more relevance to modern life.

The few of you who follow my rants and ravings on the world of business know I am socially responsible, financially conservative, and commentate on such matters with sensitivity and objectivity. So here goes: Judge Jackson was a fathead.

Microsoft has fought a rugged defence since then, and been helped by the election of an administration in the US that can palpably be bought. Judge J. has been consigned to a footnote in history, alongside Attila the Nice Guy – who was the brother of the other one and had about the same impact on history as the judge.

But the shadow of anti-trust still hangs over the Big Guys. It ruined Jack Welch's last days in power, and with mega-mergers now the name of the game all over the globe, it won't go away. Nor should it – but it needs to grow up.

I believe the public should be defended from abuse derived from misuse of monopoly power. I see evidence of such abuse in airlines, oil, media, telecommunications, banking and Tiger Woods. If we home in on Microsoft, I believe that it has occasionally entered grey areas. I think they should change some things and should be watched closely. But I do not believe that ONE consumer has suffered, directly or indirectly, by the Microsoft phenom of the last 25 years. In fact, the opposite.

They say that white, male, middle-aged ex-CEOs always write lists. Absolute Rubbish. Here are four reasons why Judge Jackson got it hopelessly wrong, and the lessons we need to apply to modern anti-trust issues.

First: capitalism is evolving, and our criteria for judging success and failure, and right and wrong, need to evolve with it. When J.P. Morgan acquired a competing railway, it was to close one down to jack the prices up and profiteer on the remaining one. That stuff was wrong, and you could mark a cross on any photo of old J.P. and submit it to a 'Spot the Exploitative Tosser' competition with a good chance for a win or place. The Sherman (Anti Trust) Acts worked to stop such abuse. That was a century ago. In the UK, the Queen Mother was avoiding her first dental cleaning.

Since then, the West has evolved into a post-industrial society. Every day we wake up and have to come to terms with mind boggling technology in our daily life, and Sting singing on the radio. It's not easy. Behind us, chronologically, Third World nations are going through their own industrial revolutions, while we are now producing and processing information, applications and services. Demand for this new stuff is all consuming. We are really just *beginning* – repeat BEGINNING – the cyber-age. We want more, faster and better stuff at our fingertips. Microsoft is not a monopoly in this world, it is still a PIONEER.

Second point: today's winning technology companies only stay ahead if they plough back billions of dollars into research and development. To invest that money you need to earn it first. Then you want some assurance that you will get some return if you keep on shovelling it in. The public benefit from this research. The technical breakthroughs of the last couple of decades have been simply staggering. Operating systems have franchised computing to the ordinary citizen and innovation has dramatically reduced prices. Microsoft lead the way on both fronts. Now, remind me of the customer abuse theory again?

Two down, two to go. Monopoly abusers are *inhibitors*. You end up having fewer railways to choose from, or fewer phone companies. Microsoft is the opposite – an *enabler*. In the last decade yours truly has evolved from a computing Luddite to somebody who uses his laptop every day, and has written and researched four books and countless columns, letters, papers and presentations on it. I am also hooked on the web, thanks to which I can track the disasters of my UK soccer team daily, and in such detail as occasionally makes me cry. The operating systems and software developed by Microsoft have been instrumental in my awakening – along with millions and millions of others. They are successful because they are GOOD, dammit. QED, they are big because they are successful. There are others, but they are less successful and therefore less big. Am I going too fast for you here, Judge Jackson?

The green-eyed monster appears in my last point. I am a Brit, and I wish Microsoft was British. I would be so proud. The only NEW global brand created by my country in the last 50 years is Virgin, lead by a man who can put his tongue out and give an impression of a haemorrhoid. In the 1950s the US gave away its consumer electronic industry to Japan – and very nearly its automobile industry as well. It's just given its mobile phone business away to … er … Finland. Oh, America – didn't you LEARN anything? When a US Olympic athlete stands on the Olympic gold medal podium, you cheer your heads off. Is there something I'm missing here? The technical world is the Olympics of capitalism. Shouldn't you *celebrate* a winner who wears your flag? It would seem strange to go up to Michael Johnson and saw his legs off.

Judge Jackson is the Kato Kaelin of the business world. His 15 minutes are now up, and he has gone. Strangely, if his ruling was ever to be upheld, I have a feeling that Bill Gates and current Microsoft stockholders might make *more* actual boring money than under the status quo. The effects of a stock split and more focus might, ironically, release more stock value. But that is not the point. Any decision to break up these New Age technology giants is wrong, and will be for some time. It fails The Test of Rightness, along with non-alcoholic beer and crash helmets for school soccer in the US.[1]

I am writing this on Windows 98. Great company, great software. Particularly the word processing. I cann*t tel(you how strongl@ I feel ab#ut th^ indefensib%# and unj*stif^able punishm*9t of excellence.

---

1 I have seen this *with my own eyes*.

MIDSUMMER NIGHT DREAMS

The dog days of summer are here again.

There is no football in the US and no soccer in the UK, so we guys are reduced to the respective delights of baseball and cricket.

I am reminded again of the many links between the two sports – starting with the length of the games. A game of cricket can actually last days. Baseball *just seems* to do the same. In addition, the combined percentage of fans of the two sports who worship fatuous, meaningless, banal statistics,[1] adds up to exactly 100% (in the UK it is 0.001%, in the US 99.999%). Finally, the daily wages of a UK cricketer

---

1 Here comes Castro Fernandez to the plate. He's batting .278 against left-handed pitchers, who operate under floodlights, in red socks, on Wednesdays, with at least three tumours from chewing tobacco on the left side of their mouths.

would buy about 50 loaves of bread, while the same for a baseball player would buy 50 loaves of emeralds.

As the summer solstice approaches, I go through my normal routine of sacrificing a small snow leopard and drinking a beaker of *lemoncello*. My mind wanders across the rooftops of the world of midsummer business:

- Gillette is disposing of its stationery businesses (Parker, Waterman pens etc.). Just 18 months ago the company had an applauded strategy of being supported by different 'pillars' of profitability. Now, that strategy looks to be one of confusing miss-focus. A not-so-gentle reminder to everyone in business – that's how *fast* it can all go wrong today. From right to wrong in a corporate heartbeat. If in doubt ask Vodaphone.
- I am starting a worldwide campaign for things that should stay black. Soccer boots (cleats) cannot be white, gold, blue or anything else in my world. It is to become a capital offence when I assume my role as Head of State (elected). Neither can London taxis be anything other than black. No New York yellow please.
- Planet Hollywood is coming out into the open again, this time heralded by some Generation-X stars. (Note to self: give the stock a miss. Again.)
- *'While both men and women are gifted for service in the church, the office of pastor is limited to men.'* Thus speaketh the proposed new language for the US Southern Baptist Convention's Faith and Message. Behold, it came to pass, in my observation, that the statement was a Crock of Shit. I wonder how Hewlett-Packard feels about this great idea? After going nowhere for years under a series of male 'pastors', the appointment of Carly Fiorina as CEO revitalized the company. Undeterred by male pastors from the whinging dregs of the HP family, she undertook to land the Grand Vision – the merge with Compaq. And achieved it against all odds. Wouldn't you love to be a fly on the wall at the interview if she applied to become a Southern Baptist?

- I wrote earlier about my resolve not to eat farmed salmon ever again. It turns out I have not eaten Salmon for about 30 years. Oh, I have eaten salmon, with a small 's', and plenty of it. But not Salmon. I was in a riverside pub in Britain's best kept secret (Wales) recently, and had a fish which had been in the river a couple of hours previously. Lean and firm, this guy had fought its way upstream over countless rapids for the honour of lying down on my plate next to some carrots and sautéed potatoes. It had been fished by rod and worm, not farmed. It was tan in colour, not orange. It was *al dente* in texture, not sludgy. It had a quite astonishing flavour. It bore no relation to the artificial, sweet rubbish that I now realize is being served and defined as salmon – and has been for more years than I care to calculate. What happened is that, to make the real thing available to more people, more often, a new fish was invented. It proved to be OK, but in the process the original DNA all but disappeared. Pondering this metamorphosis, I saw parallels in Kevin Costner – who has become a parody of himself over roughly the same time frame. I began to see the current plight of Levi Strauss in a new light.
- McDonald's has acquired Boston Market (*née* Boston Chicken). If they bought it for a unique real estate opportunity, they are brave and wise. The US market is getting mature for good, new, quick-service restaurant sites, and to pay a premium but get a bunch of them (which, by the way, also stops their competition from getting them) is bold and beautiful. If, on the other hand, they have bought it to try and resurrect the Boston Whatsit brand, they are dumb. If they have bought it to try and do both, they are dumb and dumber.
- Driving through a leafy American suburb recently, I saw a school soccer game taking place in the distance. It was a wonderful sight, taking me back to my childhood. I slowed my car down to a stop to grab a few moments' nostalgia. When I saw what I saw up close, I almost threw up. *The kids were wearing crash helmets.* This is soccer, remember, where a significant part of the game

involves heading the ball. NO, AMERICA, PLEASE, NO. Can you not get it into your collective heads that, in business, school, society and everywhere else, you cannot protect everybody from everything all the time. Potential litigation and cloying nannyism is combining to form a cholesterol that threatens to block the arteries of everything we do. Business is now suffering immensely from this syndrome. The head of the school didn't take the crash-helmet decision, it was taken (trust me on this) by a combination of some fatheaded, interfering, overprotective parent group and the school attorney. The latter should be taken out and summarily shot. Yes, I feel strongly on the subject.

- Eskimos are rumoured to have 50 different words for the types of snow they experience. Did you hear about the two Eskimos, sitting in one of their snows, chatting? One says to the other: 'Can you believe it? I hear in modern English supermarkets they have 50 different words for bread?'

LISTEN CAREFULLY: I WILL SAY THIS ONLY ONCE ...

As a result of a minor misdemeanour in the 1980s, involving the innocent misuse of a small amount of *wasabi*, a Bowie knife and a small condom, I arrived in Florida. I was made head of Burger King Corp. as part of the Federal Witness Protection Program. It proved a very creative and successful way of masking my previous identity. Surprisingly, the franchisees never spotted it.

Of course, once the Feds have you, they never let go, and recently I was 'invited' to address the senior ranks of a particularly huge government agency, which protects the nation's security. When I arrived for the gig, it took almost TWO HOURS to get in the place. Remember they invited me. At this stage I cannot tell you more. If I did, I would have to kill you.

The purpose of the session was, and I quote: *'To open our windows to non-government management thinking.'* The worthy longer-term goal is to try and increase effectiveness and efficiency in their world of zero competition and use-or-lose budget appropriations.

The reality is that there are a lot more of 'them' and a lot less of 'us' than we think. In most Western nations somewhere between a third and a half of all the checks written in the country during a year are signed by some form of government agent.

Outside that, in the cold world of the free market, there are still huge armies of people, and huge amounts of currency, in corporate cost centres which are appropriation-based, and where it is difficult to measure 'success' other than by the size of your budget, or the numbers of people who work for you or your priority in office car parking.

All these areas are experiencing increasing pressure. In the public sector, the Lords of Misrule are finally hearing the message that people accept paying taxes, but not the wastage that has been associated with spending them. Politicians on both sides of the political divide are contemplating the wisdom of a gameplan built around less taxes spent more effectively.

It is profound rubbish to say you cannot measure effectiveness and efficiency when spending big appropriation-based budgets. It is impractical to ask each such department to zero-budget every year, and it is stupid and counter-productive to introduce complex internal transfer prices for 'services'. But there are many ways to move away from the 'use-it-or-lose-it' approach. Productivity can be measured, and benchmarking against comparative departments in the free-market world can be useful. Simple measures of satisfaction – tangible and intangible – can be tracked with 'internal' customers.

It is equally dumb to infer that the public sector is not exposed to 'market forces'. If you asked the high tech companies or the fast food restaurant industry what their biggest market challenge is, they might (surprisingly) reply that it had nothing to do with customers.

Although they operate at either end of the skill-sale, they have one thing in common. Their biggest 'market' challenge is to compete in the *labour* market, where the day-to-day fight to get the right employees with the right skills at the right price is what keeps them awake at night. There is no need for the public sector to 'open their windows' to expose themselves to this market reality – in a world of full employment their ability to attract, retain and develop the talent they need to be effective and efficient is exactly the same as it is for anybody else. More importantly, success in doing this can be measured empirically. As in any other competitive arena, those who are best at it will win. Others will fall by the wayside.

Effective delegation is the delegated ability to succeed.[1] That it has no place in government organizations structured on military and/or hierarchical principles, is probably the daftest miss-assumption of the lot. Much of modern 'empowerment' theory had its roots in military and government history. There is no finer example of it than when the outnumbered English navy beat off the Spanish Armada in 1588, with the sea captains acting individually against an overall strategy agreed and signed off by the monarch. The organizational philosophy that: *'If you are below me, I am your god; if you are above me, you are mine'* never had a natural home in the public sector, although it has been adopted with deep love. It has been taken on in that sprawling organization to new levels with the invention of *assismosis* – which is the development of a career by frequently kissing the arse of your boss. But where such an attitude exists, it is – as it is always, and as it is everywhere – counter-productive and needs weeding out.

I make my escape after my speech by abseiling down the outside wall of the building, carrying Sharon Stone over my shoulder while being shot at by Bruce Willis. I ponder on the nature of these 'windows' that need to be opened. I do not believe they exist. The problem is not, therefore, that they need opening.

---

1 It is NOT, as a previous boss of mine insisted, the delegated ability to fail.

The problem is that a declining but powerful bunch of people still believe in their existence. The bigger problem is that these people clean them and polish them and paint them regularly in their imagination.

Sadly, my cover is now blown and I must choose a new identity to hide behind for the next phase of my life. I have chosen Engelbert Humperdink, and will be appearing tonight in Vegas. Please do not tell anybody.

BE LIKE MIKE ...

To be honest I have had no interest in professional boxing since that terrible night, long ago, in Madison Square Garden, when I fought Joe Louis to a draw over 15 bloody rounds. However, I have just rekindled my awareness of the 'sport'.

From my scanning of recent assorted media, three pieces of information caught my eye:

- The rat population of Manhattan is now estimated to be 70 million.
- Male life expectancy in Botswana is now 29 years.
- Mike Tyson has been licensed to fight again.

These have something in common – they all confirmed my increasing suspicion that the world is about to end.

The Tyson debacle is interesting, if only for my own amazement.

For those of you who missed it, a while back, in between spells in assorted court rooms, nightclubs, a spell in jail and some mild cannibalism, Tyson fought some unfortunate heavyweight recently in Scotland. Yes, Scotland. The whole thing lasted less than a minute. Included in that was the time needed for Tyson to pulverize his opponent, and then *knock down the referee* – who was protecting the semi-conscious victim – after the KO had been counted. Tyson then delivered a couple of final murderous blows to the pair of them and headed off into the night.

All this still didn't make for a good night's work for Iron Mike. He then threatened to eat the children of his next likely opponent.[1] Presumably, he saw this as a natural progression from having eaten part of the ear of a recent opponent.

My son and I watched the whole thing on pay-per-view, and I haven't laughed so much since Picasso died.

Nice guy, huh? It is not hard to arrive at a hope that the recent genome breakthrough should now see us abandon the search for a cure for cancer, and concentrate on producing a world that doesn't contain Mike Tysons.

It was, therefore, with some shock that I realized I'm part of the problem. To a degree so are you.

I watched the thing on TV. It was *my money* that (partly) enabled this event to go on. My money went towards his purse – i.e. rewarding the thug for his night's efforts. If there are two headlines in a newspaper: 'Mike Tyson does something crazy' and 'Small earthquake in Peru – nobody injured', which do you think I'd read? We make these guys, and, what's worse, we expect them to be nasty. What's even worse than that is we WANT them so.

Nice guys do not win, and we do not admire losers. It's not just in vicious competitions like boxing, it applies in all sports. In

1 This proved to be Lennox Lewis, who metaphorically ate Tyson's lunch instead.

England we have a tennis player, Tim Henman, who is wonderfully gifted *technically*. His game is made for Wimbledon's grass courts. But he will never win it. If he had a tenth of Tyson's child-eating mentality, he might.

This principle applies when we look to the people who run our countries. Arguably, the greatest achievement by any British Prime Minister was Churchill's refusal to give in to Hitler in 1940. Eventually, we not only survived, but were part of the winning team. It was a unique personal performance – winning against all odds. It is very easy to praise Churchill's qualities – his oratory, his articulation, his bulldog spirit. He was, however, when necessary, also the Mike Tyson of his time. At the time of the French surrender to the Germans, he personally gave the order for the British navy to destroy the French fleet to stop it falling into enemy hands. It was a pivotal decision, and a major factor in our survival and eventual victory. It may have saved millions of lives and the Hitlerization of a continent. It did, however, involve a teeny-weeny bit of 'collateral' damage: the deliberate murder of 1300 French sailors.

Nice guys do not thrive when leadership is needed in difficult times. Strangely enough, business provides the arena where this thesis is tested more than anywhere today. Almost every company – small, medium or large – is facing unprecedented trading circumstances. To be successful today, you have to institutionalize discomfort, tension and traumatic change. To relate to the Tyson circumstances, and what – in fairness – he faces in his 'profession', it must seem as though there is a huge nasty heavyweight facing you across the ring every day. The only way you CAN survive is to be nastier and dirtier. So he is, and so are many others in their world of business.

To relate this to Churchill's quandary with the French naval fleet, business leaders constantly face the need to deliberately 'sacrifice' thousands of allies – for example middle management or administrative staff – to stay competitive and win through in the end. If you don't compete, everybody dies.

Do you have to be a Tyson – a focused thug – to be a *Grand From-age* in business? No. There is a big difference between a Churchill and a Tyson, and it is one of *balance*. My observation is that a successful modern business leader must be able to take the hardest, toughest, nastiest of decisions – and live calmly with the consequences in the context of the bigger picture. But the same person cannot live in that body for 24/7. Balance becomes key. There were many days when Churchill did not have to shoot his allies. There were days to motivate, there were days to orate. There were days to create. There were days to build again. There were days to be nice. There were days to celebrate. You need to be able to do them *all*. Mike can't. Some people can. That's why there is hope.

Now then. While Tyson was doing his anti-Christ thing in Scotland, more than half a century after we blew up their navy, France won the European international soccer championship. They did this two years after winning the World Cup. England lost out in both competitions. Then we lost to them at rugby. Again.

No, I do not have an explanation.

I'M DREAMING OF A ... GREEN KETCHUP?

I quit Big Business some years ago, victim in equal part to a moment of sanity and about 19 glasses of Guinness. I had two ambitions left. My first was to know one less person every day for the rest of my life, which is on track. My second was a tad more ambitious – which was to create three global brands from scratch.

I had the chance to judge progress on my second goal recently when I saw the valuation league table of global brands. Coca-Cola was at the top – with a brand value of around $70 billion. If those of you who are clued up on this stuff would just talk among yourselves for a minute, let me just clarify what that means to those less enlightened. That figure represents the value of the *name*, and excludes the tangible assets of the company. There's is nothing in that valuation you can touch, feel or kick. It's what you would have to invest, if you launched 'Barry's Cola', to get the equivalent global awareness and reputation of Coke.

Microsoft came second, not far behind. The combined value of my three brands, agreed and reported under GAAP, was 75 cents.

The science of branding remains one of creating a product or service of distinction, then generating awareness. This, hopefully, results in a trial purchase by a customer. When that happens, you then have a chance to secure a repeat purchase, then to get more of the same, i.e. increasing the frequency of purchase. Finally, you try to secure the Holy Grail – customer loyalty.[1]

It is a simple gameplan really – but some folk go about branding in a funny way today. Here's a few to chew on:

- Arriving at a posh hotel recently, I noticed the little bar of soap in the bathroom had the words 'French Milled Soap' on the box. *French Milled Soap*. I couldn't believe that somebody had provided this wonderful luxury for free. I dropped everything and raced for the shower. I was just approaching the high bit in *Nessun Dorma*, when realization dawned. *The French don't wash*. In addition, I was born in the north of England, surrounded by mills, and they were dirty, filthy things. French? Milled? Soap? Yuk.
- For a decade or so I lived mainly in Miami. The climate and my lifestyle combined to see me in shorts or khakis jeans most days. The clothing retailer GAP has a great range of both, and I buy a particular sub-brand sporting the name: *Relaxed Fit*. I do this because those words capture my personal trouser mantra. Now, if they had *Fat Arse* written on them, which is precisely what they are, then I would avoid them like the plague.
- General Motors tried to take the branding principles behind Infiniti (motto: this car is definitely NOT a Nissan) and Lexus (motto: this one is absolutely NOT a Toyota) one step further with

---

1 Just write this paragraph down and you can skip business school.

their Saturn brand. It was to auto-buying what Woodstock was to the sixties, capturing the *zeitgeist* of the turn-of-the-millennium consumer. Car-buying was no longer to be about discounts and deals, it was to be about a relationship and mutual respect. Oops. Press the fast-forward button. On the back of disappointing sales, dealer incentives, discounting, and all the other gunk you associate with selling cars are now all the rage with Saturn. The pursuit of real market distinction can be painful. Life is safer in the pack.

- Can anybody name a distinct, branded, consumer product, that has in excess of $1 billion in global annual sales under its own name, *but that is not recognized and treated as a brand in its own right?* My old company has one. It's called the Whopper.

- The UK's Diageo, who own Burger King, also offer two examples of how wonderful branding can be when you get it right, and how frustrating it is when you get stuck on trying to take off. When (as GrandMet) they acquired the Pillsbury group over a decade ago, it included an under-performing ice-cream brand called Häagen-Dazs. Now look at it. But the group also included a brand I thought would become a world beater with GrandMet's skills behind it. It is called Green Giant, as in the Jolly Green Giant. It seemed to have everything going for it: eco/health-friendly name, massive awareness, a growth market, widespread international possibilities, and blah blah blah. A decade later? OK – but yawnsville to what I thought it might be.

- And finally, from the thinking that brought you New Coke, we present (wait for it ... drum roll) ... GREEN KETCHUP. Launched by Heinz, early in the new millennium, I can only assume the thinking behind this nightmare (do you know what it LOOKS like on your french fries?) reflects something along the following lines. Let's say current sales of red ketchup equal 100 cases. Growth is slow, with the overall ketchup market flat or even declining. The New Product Development guys have an Idea (with a big 'I'): If they introduce green ketchup, it is likely that sales of red ketchup will drop to 95 cases. However, sales of green ketchup will come in at 10 cases. Result? *Total ketchup sales of 105 cases*. Sales and profits show growth again, and maybe the total ketchup market livens up.

Now, here's my forecast for three years from now: red ketchup 100 cases, green ketchup zero. Sometimes brand managers produce stuff that is difficult to believe. I can only limit my value judgment on this beauty to a slight misquote of an old Irish maxim: *If green ketchup is the answer, it must have been a bloody daft question.*

LESSONS FROM THE GOLF PRO

Christiansted, St Croix: I am here, on a short vacation break, with nothing on my mind save the lessons golf can teach us in business. I will begin at the beginning.

Yesterday, as my wife and I stood on the first tee in the latest of our lifetime efforts to break a combined 200 for our double round, I feared the worst. The Trade Winds were coming in from the northeast in what can only be described as a very meaningful way, and this was not good news for my long, highly flighted, inaccurate game. In these sorts of conditions I am capable of hitting a shot from the tee that ends up in a position that is further away from the green than when I started. To calculate the ensuing yardage to the pin, you have to do a complicated sum that involves the square of the hypotenuse.

My initial fears were well founded. As the round progressed, with our goal disappearing, it was undoubtedly me letting the side down. For some strange reason, I seemed to be driving off from each tee into weather conditions that could only be described as light snow. This was compensated, however, by an incredible accuracy with my short putts (i.e. those less than eight inches long). This turned out to be due to the fact that I mistakenly played the first 15 holes wearing my reading glasses, and not those I wear for distance.

I stood on the sixteenth tee disheartened, but determined. This was – make no mistake – a *man's* hole. It was a long par five, dead against the wind. Head still, I let fly with my driver. At exactly the same moment the Trade Winds moved up three gears, and deposited my first ball in Venezuela. My second, provisional, ball was struck more conservatively with a three wood. It disappeared into a small rain forest system.

My wife, who played the entire round with a three wood, a five wood and a putter, then stood on the lady's tee, which seemed about a quarter of a mile nearer the green, and popped one up the middle of the fairway, cleverly going underneath the wind. We set off on our different journeys.

It was a while before we met again at the end of the hole. I played my final approach shot into the green in a bit of a hurry, out of some mangroves. My rush was not to exit the third of the world's major eco-systems I had visited during the one hole, but down to the fact that, as I lined up my chip shot, I was being eyed by (I think) a rare blue-spotted anaconda, relishing the thought of something other than turtle's eggs for lunch.

As I arrived at the green, my wife was standing over her ball, six feet from the flagstick. She promptly sank the putt. With great deliberation, she looked back down the fairway, mouthed some numbers to herself, and announced that she was sure that was her fourth shot. She also asked, innocently, if that was one of those 'falcons'. I told her that it was, indeed, a 'birdie', and my silence as we walked to the next tee was a thing of beauty.

I had much the same feeling of frustration when we decided we had to can a good ad campaign in Burger King a few years ago. The frustration was not from the failure. The frustration was from one of our franchisees coming up to me afterwards and telling me that he'd *known all along* it wouldn't work. This was a guy whose contribution to the system was to run restaurants with a standard of hygiene that offered the diner about a 50:50 chance of avoiding anthrax.

Tiger Woods dominates golf today in a way that is rare in any modern sport. He regularly makes the world's great courses – such as St Andrews in Scotland and Pebble Beach in California – look like a holiday resort's Crazee Golf set-up. Can his success teach us anything?

You bet.

Successful golfers, more than any other sports folk, can be paralleled with business people. You need technique and technology in golf, as you do in business. But after that it's more mind-control than physique. It is tough to liken a business challenge to Michael Johnson running a 200-metre race in less than 20 seconds, but a top golfer, using his or her *mental make-up* as a weapon, has some similarity with business.

These folk have one magnificent ability that we could all use. It is present in all top golfers, and always has been. If it is not present, success will not be sustainable over the medium or long term. It is the ability to concentrate totally on the next shot, and *only* the next shot. It is the ability to close out memories of the sad failure OR glorious success that occurred with the last one. It is the ability to avoid rehearsing the victory speech when you are six up with two to play. It is the ability to address the next challenge with a clear and uninfluenced mind. There is absolutely no static in their focus-system.

In my observation, very few people in leadership positions in business have this talent. Decision-making and actions are corroded by events and experiences from the past, shaped by the what's happening today and battered and blown about by a whole host of possible 'what-ifs?' in the future.

This wondrous myopia is talent I never had. I get *deflected* up the wahoo. When it comes to being curious, I have a nose like a blind cobbler's thumb. It is full of holes and supersensitive to smells, which it always wants to follow. This goes some way to explaining why, when I transfer the skills I have to the golf course, I visit rare eco-systems and never score Falcons.

It may also go some way to explaining why my writing tends to occupy the lower slopes of the appropriate bookshops.

LEARNING THE HARD WAY

Between the ages of 13 and 16, I spent a heady proportion of my waking hours in a rather unusual physical position. It was a standing pose, although bent forward from the waist up. My hands rested just above my knees. This was the correct position to be thwacked on the butt by my school headmaster and assorted teachers and prefects. It was the standard and accepted punishment for my many and varied school misdemeanours.

The weapons used were either a length of cane (headmaster) or various gym shoes and sneakers (the other bastards). This was before the days you could report such treatment to your parents and, if you lived in the US, then sue the school for $80 million. If my dad found out, he would usually add a couple more thwacks with whatever was to hand to make sure the lesson got home.

During one of these Arse-Tattoos – and I can't remember the actual face of the person responsible (remember – I was facing the other way) – the perpetrator accompanied his rhythmic thwacking with the immortal words: 'What you have done here, Gibbons, *fails the test of rightness.*'

I have remembered those words. From the time I joined business, barely a day has passed without me looking at some activity, or evaluating some behaviour, and deciding it failed that test. I dedicated a whole chapter in a recent book of mine to the subject, and I'm never short of new material. Here are two beauties:

To get the new millennium off to a good start, the leaders of the (economically) developed nations met in Okinawa, Japan, at the so-called G8 Summit. Yet another Dronefest. That's fine. Along with the six billion people on the planet I ignored it.

It transpires, however, that the bill for this 'meeting' was the equivalent of *seven hundred million dollars* when it was totalled up in all its forms and currencies.

Now, let me open my own kimono here and confess a couple of things. In times gone by I have been known to push the boat out at corporate meetings. I have had dinner appetizers that consisted of lobster thermidor, washed – sorry, flooded – down with Dom Perignon vintage champagne. I have quaffed (the only word for it) 1912 Malmsey. My only excuse is that I was older then, and I'm younger than that now. But the biggest challenge I ever had was to get the accounts department to rub vanishing cream on a couple of grand. How, in the name of Adam's sperm count, do you spend $700 million on a *meeting*?

Here's where this event failed the test of rightness. Leadership is about giving off signals. When you are laying people off, good leaders do not go to the bathroom in stretch limos. They do not use the corporate jet to fly their dogs to be groomed. In the same way, if you are dealing with Third World poverty, world political leaders should not blow the price of a major international health initiative on the meeting itself. It sickens and alienates any rational audience. It gives the protesters huge dumps of ammo. It makes the leaders look hollow. It dilutes the credibility of the exercise. It is wrong.

At about the same time, to get the new millennium off to a real flyer, a US jury socked the US tobacco industry for a *$145 billion* punitive damage award. THERE! Let THAT be a lesson to you! A second, parallel and massive, failure of the test of rightness.

I bow to no one in my detestation of the people who have lead the tobacco industry over the last half century, and who have attempted to mislead the public as to the addictive and health damaging properties of nicotine. But *they* are my enemies. Not the tobacco farmers, workers, investors and distributors. Like it or not, they work within the existing law of the land. Nor are my enemies the people who benefit from the tax revenues from tobacco, which underpin huge public spending programmes.

Frankly, you would have to have been deaf, dumb and blind for the last 50 years not to have realized that nicotine was a) bad for you and b) addictive. I understood that with crystal clarity in 1958 after watching a black and white film in school. The film was targeted at the likes of me, and achieved exactly the result it sought – namely a lifetime of abstinence from tobacco on my part. I made my personal choice – but that was MY choice. My enemies are not the people who also understood that, but still made a free (and lawful) choice to smoke. They traded off the benefits (as they defined them) against the risks. Yet it is ALL these people that this award will punish if smoking is driven underground.

The failure of the test of rightness is NOT the amount of money[1] – although that is stupid in itself. Did you notice what happened to tobacco industry stock prices when the news was published? Nothing, that's what. Investors know that the amount is so ludicrous, the companies won't pay a penny of it. So the whole thing is a load of *bollo.*

---

1 It's a recurring theme in this book, I know – but do any of you remember when a billion (i.e. a thousand million) dollars or pounds was a lot of money? When did it become Chump Change? And how did I miss out?

The real failure of the test of rightness is who gets punished. Humungous damages would mostly hit the people listed above, who are not the enemy. Neither are the corporations involved. Fining the Philip Morris Corporation is like blaming something called 'Germany Inc.' for the holocaust. Germany Inc. wasn't to blame. There was a select bunch of identifiable *people* who knew exactly what they were doing, and who could not, and should not, have been defended by the concept of limited liability by virtue of belonging to an 'organization'. Nuremberg proved that we can identify and bring such individuals to justice. There have been a bunch of like people in the tobacco industry over the last few decades, who have knowingly attempted to mislead the consuming public. They are identifiable individuals. They are the enemy. We should haunt them and hound them as we do war criminals.

For these evildoers, ten of the best from my old school headmaster would not be enough. And I say that with reverence because I once survived such an onslaught. My backside looked like a map of the London Underground for weeks.

WHEN DILBERT WAS FUNNY ...

One of my early successes was to invent modern PR at the age of 17.

Like most late male teenagers in the gloomy north of England at the time, I spent the whole of every weekend in pursuit of Girls Who Might. My weaponry was extensive – a large handful of Brylcreem, an extensive application of orange (it seemed) coloured Clearasil and regular hormonal explosions. None of the Girls Who Might ever did, of course. Which left you facing an audience of your school peers on Monday morning, forced to fabricate a plausible story, usually R-rated, based on zero substance. *This is the exact principle on which modern PR is based.*

My school buddy, let's call him Sam because that is his name, experienced success in a different field. Always athletic, he was identified as a potential professional soccer player, and whisked off to join a top club when he was about 16. When I saw him again a few weeks later, his legs had metamorphosed into oak trees. He became a regular back-up for the first team, where the starter in his position was an England international. This guy helpfully broke his leg in the semi-final of England's knockout soccer cup in 1966, and my buddy took his place in the Cup Final at Wembley, in front of 100,000 people. This occurred at the ripe old age of 17.

To this day we remain pals. A million beers and about 100 joint pounds later, we pondered recently a life where the undisputed peak arrives before you are 20. The shadow of that peak can last a long time and reach a long way. It can be tough to work and live in it.

In English we have an expression, and I don't know if it translates into American, but I'll try. It says: *give me success – but not too much, and not too early.*

Following this line of thought, you can arrive at some disturbing judgments. Perhaps Mozart did not die soon enough? Should we allow kids like Kerri Strug, the four-year-old US gymnast at the Atlanta games, to compete for Olympic gold medals? Wouldn't it be wonderful if Dilbert's funniest cartoons were still to come?

The latter is a fascinating case study. I have nothing against Scott Adams, the creator of Dilbert and his dysfunctional cronies. When they first hit the newspapers I loved them. The little strip captured the *zeitgeist* and the idiocies of the modern workplace. I identified with it. I was both a victim and a cause of the lunacy he captured brilliantly. Along with a zillion other people, I couldn't get enough. This may have actually proved to be part of the problem because we then got enough. Did we ever. Books, merchandising, total coverage – it was everywhere. Today, I still read it – but it feels as though it's been hard work to produce, and it's hard work to digest. Contrast that with Charlie Brown, who took over the world's psyche slowly and gracefully – to the extent that, even after all those years, it was only death that stopped Charles Shultz reaching a peak that was still ahead of him.

Too much success, too soon. A bad thing. Which brings me to the late and unlamented dotcom company phenomenon. The cull has started, with failures and mergers now hitting the headlines more than the earlier, astonishing, stories of paper riches. The problem now is not that there have been so many failures – but that there have still not been enough. But the revolution is real, and winners will emerge. The science and technology will be new, but victory will come on the back of the old conventional principles – if your website has clear distinction, and your target consumers are aware of it, you will prosper.

There may, however, be something different this time. *This might be the first generation of start-up business survivors that won't be able to handle success.*

Traditionally, starting a business is a grind. You are usually undercapitalized, under-resourced and starved of any credit. You have to torture every discretionary penny you spend. Overhead is an enemy. You understand every nuance of your product pricing and margin structure. Money available for marketing is measured in hundreds, not millions, of whatever currency you swim in. But if you do survive – and I have seen the success rate estimated as low as 5% – you have these lessons learned. Usually, you are ready.

Contrast that with a dotcom that survives this cull. With a management team that has no sense for these values. Burn rate? Marketing funds? Well, when the cupboard was empty they would normally just phone the investors and pull in another few million. Creating awareness? It seemed a good idea to book an advertising spot on the Super Bowl show at a couple of million dollars a throw – excluding media production costs. Pricing? Margins? Overheads? *Who cares*? They were not expected to be profitable. At a time when a traditional start-up company might start to forget about survival and start to think about growth, these guys might find themselves in a secondary mess – caused by their own shallow skill base and inadequate sense of value.

I would not, however, want you to think all is lost in the dotcom world. I do not want you convinced there can be no more winners. That there can be no more humungous wealth creation. Far from it. In fact, I just happen to have a guaranteed winner myself, targeted at the very lucrative 17-year-old-male market in the north of England. It is called GirlsWhoMight.com. It is updated every Friday night.

Write to me for an investment prospectus.

CHAMPAGNE FIRST, PLEASE

We will now examine the intriguing world of brand sponsorship, and why it may be necessary to shoot your Chairman's spouse.

Any person, or company, that sells a product or service, is in the branding business. It does not even have to be a commercial (i.e. for profit) enterprise – one of the best examples of the science being the UK's 'Red Nose' annual charity day of recent years.

The successful accumulation of brand equity – the value placed on the reputation and awareness of your brand name alone – can now easily surpass the value of any tangible assets on your balance sheet. It can be worth tens – even hundreds – of millions of pounds in its own right, but it can take decades and vast amounts of marketing spend to get there. Sponsorship is one of many tools used by brand mangers to build brand equity.

Early in the new millennium, I watched the admirable American cyclist Lance Armstrong win the Tour de France. At the time of writing, he did this for the fourth time in a row. Now then, I bow to no man in my admiration for anybody who wins this particularly gruelling event,[1] but I want to look at it through a different pair of eyes.

Let's play around a bit, and imagine we are a Frenchman, keen on cycling, standing by the side of the road, in a tiny village called *Vermin-sur-Fromage*, in the mountains of the *Massif Central*, waiting for the race to come through. I'm stretching my French here, but I suspect his thoughts might run something like this:

> *Alors, c'est tres hot. Attendez, ici comes le race! Sacre Bleu, l'American, monsieur Armstrong, est up front. Il est something else, n'est-ce pas? Quel dommage, apres his bike il y a beaucoup de cars et trucks. Q'est-ce-que written dans le side de each of them? Ah, je see now. 'US Postal service'. Fuck – moi, cet service must be tres bon. Le next time je poste une lettre, je will use them. Pas de doubt.*

This is where we hit a snag. The magnificent US team, led by Armstrong, were sponsored by the US Postal Service. The problem is that *Jean*, our Frenchman (that's his name, really), along with the 300 million Europeans who care about cycling, cannot change their buying behaviour and substitute the US Postal Service for the one they are lumbered with in their country. The three people in the US who are interested in European cycling might be really impressed, but that's a long, slow way to build brand equity in your key market.

It is a fine example of Dumb Sponsorship, or DS as it's known. DS is normally the result of the company chairman, *or his/her spouse*, pushing the big discretionary brand sponsorship dollars towards

---

1 In fact I hold my hands up to ANY sporting champion – the reason being that if I had £1 for every sporting success I achieved I would be able to buy myself a small sherry.

a sport or event that a) they follow avidly and b) will enable them to mingle with the stars and *maybe even sign autographs.* One of the strange phenomena of big business success is that, even at its highest level, it doesn't bring the celebratory status of entertainment or sports stardom. So they figure out a way to buy that. Hence the embarrassing sight of white, 50-something CEOs, playing golf with the Big Golf Names in the pro-am of their brand's sponsored TV golf tournament, and mumbling through 30 seconds of a network TV interview on a Sunday afternoon.

Sponsorship can be effective in building brand awareness and imagery. But any spending on it needs to be targeted ruthlessly just as it is for any other marketing budget. The effectiveness and efficiency of the cash (and management time) invested can be measured, and it should be tracked and reviewed empirically. It is NOT good enough to lump it under the loosey-goosey label of 'customer relations' just because you invite some existing and/or potential buyers to the event. Would you lose these customers if you didn't sponsor the event? I think not – and there are many more cost effective ways in which you can secure repeat purchase and customer loyalty. Of course, they might involve hard work.

The US Postal Service and the golf-star chasers and celebrity wannabes provide us with the three golden DON'Ts of sponsorship:

- Don't let the Chairman or his/her spouse near the sponsorship budget.
- Point it somewhere near your target market (and DEFINITELY NOT France).
- Golf is spoken for. Don't do it. It's Done. It's a dead parrot.

I don't want you thinking, however, that there are no more exciting sponsorship opportunities. In fact, for all you aspiring brand managers out there, I have an outstanding opportunity for you. I am bringing back, into the public domain, a sport that was all the rage in pre-war Hungary – the *Budapest Pentathlon*. World War II stopped it, but I am determined to see it back where it belongs, in the summer Olympics. Even I couldn't invent this – so take it as gospel. It is a bit like the Pentathlon, inasmuch as it has five events that every competitor must complete. The rules are simple – you walk three miles, run three miles, ride a horse for three miles, make love to three women, and drink three bottles of champagne.

Now, in a world of equal opportunity, I accept that, in the modern version, the 'three women' bit will have to be adapted to reflect equal opportunity and same-sex relationships, but that is a detail. The real excitement lies in the secondary rules. To qualify for a tournament, you have to do it all in less than three hours. But here's the real beauty of the event – *you can choose your own sequence.*

Forget 'Survivor' and 'Millionaire'. This is made for TV. I am leading the movement to see it back in its rightful place in the planet's sporting calendar, and you may write to me with huge sponsorship offers.

One additional detail: after a short but pointed domestic debate last night, I have agreed with my wife I will assume the role of our team's non-playing captain.

ALL THAT USELESS BEAUTY

Flying into England recently, I smile as I remember one of my early triumphs. In 1962, after several beers and a not insubstantial wager, I entered the Miss UK beauty contest. I was slimmer then, and my lips a little fuller – and the effect of some tactical applications of borrowed make-up and two rugby socks pushed down the front of my T-shirt was electrifying. History records I won with ease, although many say it wasn't a vintage year. I should also point out that this was before they had to make short speeches. I went on to be placed fifth in Miss Universe.

The message for all is that sometimes beauty hides something darker. As we land at London Heathrow, the chilling sight of a Concorde taking off echoes that thought. Early in the new millennium, the glorious Flagship of the French and British national airlines had been brought to a standstill on the back of the horrendous image of a fireball crashing into a hotel near Paris. It was an image that was captured on every TV screen in the world, and the disaster saw the whole fleet grounded while they sorted out what went wrong.

When Concorde was originally launched, I worked for a major oil company in the UK. I wasn't directly involved in the jet fuel part of the business, but a couple of my buddies were wrapped up in what seemed like a terribly complicated set of issues surrounding fuelling and passenger pay-load before it finally began to operate commercially. Their mutterings were to the effect that it would never make money. So I was suspicious of it from Day One.

Soon afterwards it became clear that it was not going to be able to fly supersonically over land, as the populations involved were, understandably, less than enthused about the unannounced enormous bangs as it broke the sound barrier. When, as a result of being frightened out of your skin, you've spilt hot coffee on your groin for the sixth time, it becomes irksome. Particularly in those counties where you can't sue McDonald's.

It became clear that the future of mainstream commercial air flight was going to be about a low overhead operation getting 400 people from London to Florida in nine hours for a few hundred pounds each, rather than a high overhead gameplan getting 100 people from London to New York in three hours for several thousand.

It also became clear that the future of mainstream commercial flight was NOT going to be built around what was *technically possible*, but around common sense and economics. Men in white coats, the senior executives of the airlines involved, and the representatives of the governments who had sunk oodles of taxpayers' cash in pursuit of being Technically Groovy howled their derision. Common sense, they said (some of them in French), was a condom on the penis of progress. But common sense ruled. In this case, the best was deemed the enemy of the good.

Quite clearly, from that moment on, there was never going to be a second generation of Concordes. Maybe in a couple of centuries from now, when other paradigms change, its time may come again – but in the meantime, in the long-term fleet planning of the major airlines, Concorde and supersonic flight achieved Dead Parrot status. Which left an open question: what to do with the dozen or so that had been (expensively) built and commissioned by British Airways and Air France? It was around this time we began to hear the word *Flagship*.

Concorde would assume the role of image-maker for the two airlines. By keeping them flying on selected high-profile routes, going over the top with the wine list, offering things called *goujons* for lunch, targeting rich or expense-accounted movers and shakers for customers and linking Concorde imagery with the two brand names on the hour every hour, the two airlines made a statement to the world. *We're simply the best*. And when you fly with us on YOUR terms, Mr Average Customer, and you fly another one of our planes, and you are delayed, over-booked, hassled and fed garbage in the back of it – we'd like you to remember what we are REALLY about.

In 1988, as somebody else was thoughtfully paying, I overcame my suspicions and flew it. Flagship-smagship. Big deal.[1] But it was a pretty-looking plane.

The idea of having a Flagship for your brand is not limited to the travel industry. It is common for a luxury goods brand to have a dedicated retail store on Madison Avenue or in The Ginza. In this case, it's called a Brand 'Flagship Store', although it doesn't fly or sail anywhere. Manufacturers like Sony have them. I suspect the Virgin mega-store in Times Square is indirectly aimed at selling airline tickets as well as CDs. Even in Burger King there used to be a mentality that said, if you were going to enter into a new market (particularly internationally), you should consider making the first

1 I flew on the same flight as Tony Curtis. That is all you need to know and, surely, all you want to know about Concorde.

one an enormous (unprofitable) emporium, in a prime location, to announce your arrival.

Flagships are all over the place, in many businesses. And they are universal poppycock. Their role in society is like a man carrying a dog. They can look pretty, but you can't respect them.

Hardly any of them make money, and most of them live by the weakest of commercial justifications (e.g. writing the operating deficit off to the PR budget). They do the wrong things for the wrong reasons. They are deflective. Fully-costed (and I do mean FULLY costed)[2] the economics never make sense. They become corporate hobbies. And when they go wrong, they work the OTHER way – they bring high-profile grief to your brand. When they fail or close – or in the worst case plunge from the sky on fire – at a stroke the negatives more than wipe out any accumulated positives.

The only exceptions I can think of are in pop music. As I reluctantly dab on my lipstick and again push my rugby socks down my shirt-front prior to going on stage, I reflect that, under my new stage name of Posh Spice, I am currently Britain's Flagship.

2 A buddy of mine used to have an unofficial measure for costing this kind of project. When all the financial data was established, which often used to be skewed to make the thing look good, he would then insist on another measurement. He called it Return on Management Time Invested. I pass the idea on without charge. Use it in appropriate circumstances, and you will be astonished at the truth that emerges.

LIGHTS OUT, PLEASE

I had a bad fall from a ladder recently. It happened while my wife and I were finishing the monthly video we make for the Playboy Channel. I ended up on the floor in a slowly expanding red puddle, which was, unfortunately, blood. My wife was so shocked she spilled nearly all the custard.

I was in my Miami home at the time, so it was off to the local hospital, where I arrived with my foot encased in a plastic bag from Publix supermarket. I didn't know this when I put it on, but this bag was poorly designed to do the job required of it – containing, as it did, tiny air holes. Consequently, the blood kept leaking out onto the floor in the hospital reception. The only reason I tell you this is in case any of you want a scheme that gets you seen QUICKLY when you arrive at the A&E ward. Take my word for it – this does.

The hospital casualty team was great. I was sewn up in no time and dispatched back into the world, complete with a leg cast and crutches. The latter were new, and given to me still in the wrapping.

Two weeks later, and I was un-stitched and back in business. Without thinking about what I was doing, I offered my 'almost new' crutches back to the hospital. It just seemed the obvious thing to do. I'd finished with them, they were taking up room and, surely, somebody could use them. They looked at me as though I had landed from Mars. I think they thought I was trying to *sell* them back. Their basic message to me was that my insurance company had 'bought' them for me, they had no process to take them back, and if I didn't want them, the dumpster was over there. When my insurance bill came through, they were itemized as more than $100.

I lived in the US for 11 plus years and loved it and the people. I still do. There are, however, two things I have never come to terms with in the US: the ability of business associates to lie to you without any personal discomfort, and the WASTAGE of almost every resource.

In my Burger King days, I used to look at the food left on people's plates, which was then trashed, and ponder at the existence of soup kitchens in the neighbourhood. When we opened a big new location in South Korea, the unit manager got into trouble for passing 'old' burgers out of the back window. These were the burgers that had gone past their time on the heat tray, which we would normally trash. He was not making a quick buck – his defence was that it was obscene to trash these when people were starving. So he passed them out of the back window. Quite. None of us knew where to look for a moment or two.

To this day none of my family has got used to the portion size in most US family restaurants. Basically, a good meal is one you cannot see over. The idea that we can take the surplus home in a little paper bag hasn't caught on with us either – once I've had my bath full of *linguine alla vongole* on Sunday, I don't want to see it again on Monday.

The West may soon face its biggest fuel oil crisis since the Arab–Israeli wars. The War on Terrorism has many unknown twists and turns to go, most of which could affect the Middle East. Oil supplies are already tight, and prices, following the eternal law of supply and demand, are high. Balance of payments deficits are going (negatively) off the graph. Distribution-based businesses are suffering, and we may or may not be in a recession. There is a lot of uncertainty about, but The Enemy is clear – it's Johnny Foreigner again.

In the US, George Dubya proposes a solution that involves drilling in Alaska. Meanwhile, his country's 'de-regulated' energy policy is shipwrecked by Enron. To help all this, the US pulls up the drawbridge and refuses to join in international programmes that could address energy issues at macro level – like the Kyoto protocol.

Everybody has a proposed solution. We demand OPEC produce more. In the US the government is under pressure to release oil reserves. Blah blah blah. It doesn't take much, however, to notice all the proposed political remedies are *supply side* solutions. They are proposed ways to service the West's ballooning energy needs, while keeping the price down. It is exactly the same mentality that saw my new crutches put on the dumpster – the question is not how we can use the crutches we have more effectively, but how can we ensure the constant supply of new ones? Nobody has the *cojones* to push for *demand side* solutions – that the West should look in the mirror, take stock of itself and *reduce its demand for energy.*

Let's go back to the issue of wastage. I have seen estimates that 5% of the West's electricity usage is now attributed to computers, TVs, videos (etc.) that are not being used but *which are* permanently *on stand-by.* Let me put an observation to you. It is my belief we could rub vanishing cream on the whole 'energy crisis' by reducing only *unnecessary* resource usage – and not even all of that.

I know thousands of families and business folk in both the UK and USA. I suspect that 70% of them could reduce their usage of food, water, dedicated real estate and utility energy by 5% without NOTICING. I further suspect that it could be as much as by 10–15% without any tangible hardship.

If you remove food and water from the above, I believe exactly the same premise applies to business – it could reduce energy usage substantially without much hardship. Now, if we could find leaders who would be prepared to ride hard on us to do that, we would have some of the most effective ones in our history.

Of course, everything is relative. In the UK alone, we bring different dimensions to the problem. The vulnerability of our fuel situation has moved to a point beyond crisis.

For years we have defended our independent nuclear weapons, and we have an army, navy and airforce which have worldwide respect. But the message we gave early in the new millennium to any potential aggressor nation or terrorist is that you don't need to take on *any* of these to roll us over. All you do is drive a rickety old farm tractor from Wales up to the front gate of the oil refinery at Ellesmere Port. Then you park it, and stand by it with a sign complaining about fuel taxes and prices. Within three days, the country will be at a standstill. No ifs, buts or maybes – it really happened.

Somebody needs to start the ball rolling if we are to move to a new age of responsibility. We need reduced resource usage and more recycling. I will lead. I have, on offer, a pair of slightly used aluminium crutches. They have had one careful owner, and have less than 40 yards on the clock. I will take £50 pounds, and not a penny less.

AMAZINGLY GRACELESS

The Chinese gangs who, along with the international pharmaceutical industry, underwrite the modern Olympics, are (coincidentally) the same ones that pay me a pleasing monthly retainer. They ask me to do an in-depth review on the whole Olympic concept – before Sydney is a lost memory and we become locked into key decisions for Athens.

There are a number of important questions to be answered, notably:

- When will it be appropriate to formally include the Nike 'swoosh' into the Stars and Stripes flag? Will it eventually go 'midst the Stars or the Stripes? (A number of design alternatives have tested well in focus groups.)

- Once we have used the existing committed locations, should we just rotate the Olympic venue up and down the key cities of the US which are on Eastern Standard Time? That way we avoid all the inconvenience of time zones and tape delays for NBC – who seem, after all, to own and control the Olympics. We simply can't go on pissing off these poor programme producers and advertisers.

- The Big Question: is it possible to trace the exact date when America stopped being a class act? When it donned designer sunglasses, and became ugly, bloated, gloating, preening and insensitive – as exemplified by the post-race antics of the winning men's relay team at Sydney?

Sadly, the few notable (and glorious) remaining exceptions simply prove this new rule.

I travel to New England – because the answer to these burning questions must be here. It must have its roots in that terrible and mistaken day when America ceased to be British.

Very quickly, I find encouraging evidence that *none of it may have actually happened.*

So that I could go right back to the genesis, I drove the short distance to Plymouth Rock. Clearly, no potential 'Americans' could possibly have landed there and disembarked from a boat. There is no wheelchair access and the whole thing is outside ADA regulations. So that's all *bollo.*

As for the Revolution, the whole thing looks invalid to me and should be stripped from the history books. I have studied local archives from the time in question, and there is clear evidence Paul Revere tested positive for neophosterosophenoline, a performance-enhancing (and banned) substance. There is no other explanation that supports the ridiculous improvement in his times for the riding-your-horse-while-screaming-event. And his defence that it came from an over-the-counter nasal spray to combat the plague (and boils) is pathetic.

Nearly a decade ago, I was delighted to attend an evening in Pittsburgh to honour Tony O'Reilly, the Irish marketing genius who ended up heading the mighty Heinz empire. He is a master after-dinner speaker, and held us all in the palm of his hand as he addressed us in his lilting Irish brogue. I was new to the US, and listened intently[1] as he attributed the enormous strengths of this nation to the ironic fact that it was borne out of defeat. Most nations attribute their historic birth to the circumstances where Nation A conquers Nation B in war. They are, therefore, borne out of victory. The modern US, however, was born from the opposite, with oppressed and defeated peoples pouring in to the country from west and east. O'Reilly saw this as the source of a great strength. The nation that emerged had a unique person-to-person *sensitivity* for the plight and position of fellow humans.

I agreed with his historical analysis. I agreed with him on the night he spoke. I can only offer qualified agreement now.

The Olympic spirit is about more than the result. It is about *how* you carry yourself, and what you stand for. Sadly, for every class act wearing US colours, there were many who saw themselves as the centre of some grimy universe. Athletes who had no respect for opponents they had beaten, or who had beaten them. They behaved like graceless cretins.

This recent trend is evident in business. In sectors where megamergers have become the *de rigueur* route to survival and prosperity, there has been a loss of soul and grace. Richard Branson once described the three brand attributes of Virgin as *fun, innovation and great value*. He's having a hard time these days as a businessman, and personally I find him a pain, but that's still a sound summary of the Virgin brand personality.

If you were to undertake the same exercise today for the huge drug and oil companies, the giant telecommunications conglomer-

---

1 I had to listen intently. I was awarding him his Oscar-equivalent, and had shared the top table with the great man. As a result I was gently pissed, and had to concentrate really hard to ingest the speech.

ates and the global financial institutions – what three would you come up with? How about: *Remote*? *Self-centred*? *Insensitive*? Now go back and link that to those punks who masqueraded after their winning relay. Zoom in on Amy Dykester, the Amazing Graceless, that corpulent American swimmer who kindly spat in the lane of her chief rival before the race, and see how all the pieces are coming together. It's an ugly jigsaw.

The roots to all this, I am convinced, lie in the deep waters of Boston Harbour. When Mr Otis coined the hunting-call of the Revolution as no 'Taxation Without Representation', he sewed the seeds of future chaos. In the act of pouring the tea into the harbour, we find the roots of the fall from grace. You see, TWR is back again – only this time it's called a Green Card. You can live and earn a living in America. You pay taxes to Uncle Sam, but you can't vote for anything or anybody. And it is official US fiscal policy.

I post my report off to Beijing, and my wife and I walk down to Boston Harbour. We decide to rebel. We must re-establish the US as a class act – the world needs nothing less. Slowly, we pour our Starbucks in the dark green water, and I read aloud my Declaration of Re-Colonization. It is the only way back to grace for the US.

Apart from a rather lethargic seagull, nobody seems interested.

R U THERE? THIS IS 4 U

I have been back in England only three days when I receive an emergency text message on my cellular phone. I must report at once to the Palace.

For almost a quarter of a century I have been waiting for the call. Under the Emergency Powers Act of 1726, it was deemed that, in cases of extreme national crisis, power and decision making would need to be removed from the hands of politicians and given to a carefully selected team of raw power and substance. In these modern times it has been decreed that these will be chosen and lead by me.

As we gather solemnly in the back room of The Clinton Arms, the new theme pub and cigar emporium near Marble Arch, I cannot help but notice the tense expressions on the faces of my carefully selected team – Elton John is pale, Elizabeth Hurley is almost white beneath her perfect make-up and Prince Charles' ears are twitching. The latter is an awesome sight, and keeps blowing our agenda papers on to the floor.

His Worship, the Master of the Rolls, briefs us on the crisis. And what a crisis it is. As a nation, it threatens the very core of our being.

The English language is under threat.

A new study has indicated that the extensive use of e-mail and text messaging by school-age kids has lead to the creation of a kind of E-pigeon English. Basic principles of spelling, punctuation and grammar are being ignored. These kids write u instead of you, thru instead of through, and str8 instead of straight. There are no capital letters or paragraphs. IMHO universally means In My Humble Opinion. The more sensitive and distant parents should sit down before they read the next bit – but there is now not a teenager alive, who is on-line or has a cell-phone, who does not know how to use punctuation to 'draw' the genitalia of both sexes (trust me).

The whole emotional tone of a communication, instead of being articulated in seven paragraphs of purple prose with 50 adverbs, is now covered by ending with a:-) or a:-(

If you think that's cool, in England, most of the kids use the phone keyboard to do all this – *and use only their left hand*.

Now then. The world of business is forecast to grind to a halt as a result of all this.

I find myself torn. I owe a duty to England to sort this out, but I am growing to love this new generation and their exciting way of doing things. It is not actually the generation immediately behind me, but the one following that who are leading the way. They have signalled that they are not going to vote in political elections, which is a wonderfully positive gesture. They don't just accept change and reinvention, they relish it. Nothing fazes them. They are actually wonderfully gifted, creative and extensive communicators. Technology has no – I repeat NO – fears for them.

Just what the hell are we supposed to be defending? The language we have is ludicrous, and it is high time we blew it up and started again. This time we don't want a load of old cobblers like *Esperanto*, because that just confuses us even more. We need a universal language that is quick to communicate and absolutely understandable – and these kids have done it for us. We mustn't try to fight it – there is no force as irresistible as an idea whose time has come.

If you landed from Mars, and you'd just bought the Planet Earth, you'd expect some sort of Operating Manual – and in it you'd expect a section on how to speak English. You would be confronted with NINE different pronunciations of the letters 'ough'. When I stand on a golf tee, I usually put my ball in something called the rough. Now, it seems to me that word should actually be spelled ruff, to match the thing I have on the end of my shirt sleeve, which is called a cuff. But, no, the thing on the golf course is spelled rough. Which brings us to the word through, which, paying heed to the aforesaid lesson with rough, should clearly be pronounced thruff. I mean, come on.

In the early years of the Age of Aquarius – my college years – we went through a similar upheaval. This time it was in mathematics. During my earlier schooling, the *process* of getting to the end result was very important. If you didn't know *how* to calculate, then any sum was beyond you. Then chip technology put a basic calculating machine within reach of everybody, and the whole paradigm changed. Logarithms and slide rules disappeared. Instead of producing worksheets showing your long divisions, you pressed a button and got it right 100% of the time. The purists hated it, but the world didn't come to an end. Far from it. We found we could use mathematics as a means to an end, rather than as an end in itself.

What the world found out was that if there is a faster way of doing something, it will usually win. It found out that if there is a better way of doing something, that way will usually take over. And it found out that if there is a better AND faster way, the old way is dead. We found out again what history has told us repeatedly – that the world does not want to know about the pains of labour, the world wants to hold the baby.

IMHFO,[1] so it will be with the English language. I have no doubt that the explosion in the use of keyboard text communication, from now on a part of the daily business and domestic lives of millions of people, will change the style and structure of our language profoundly. It is to be welcomed, by business in particular. What you communicate is important, not how – and these kids are already leaving us for dead with the effectiveness and efficiency of their communication habits. Once again, we – the old guard – are reduced to defending the indefensible.

I dismiss the meeting. There is no crisis. *Au contraire,* something wonderful is happening.

Later, I e-mail the Queen and resign. Nothing personal, I tell her, I've just had enuf. Thanx anyway. CU L8A:-)

---

1 This is a slight variation on the acronym outlined earlier in this piece. Work it out yourself.

LOAVES AND FISHES

Like most journalists, I have my own sources in the Vatican. I often refer to them as my 'Deep Throats', but the joke seems to escape them. A few weeks ago, two of them, acting quite separately, but in a panic, e-mailed me to give me a 'heads up' warning on a terrifying pending announcement. I rushed to Italy to try and avert disaster, but my personal plea remained unheeded. A senior theologian of the Catholic Church issued a statement condemning the fast food industry – my old stamping ground.

I quote the translated version of his historic epistle:

The sense of community is absent in fast food. It is not a model for Catholics.

Now, I don't want to get off on a rant here, but this is a load of Imperial *Bollo*.

I should declare, at the outset, that I am not religious in the normal sense. I am a Paranoid Agnostic, not believing in a God as such, but believing there is a force out there, *which is pursuing me*. My thoughts on Catholicism, specifically, are those of anybody with a healthy mind on a religious Establishment that has only just ratified Copernicus and is still uneasy with Darwin.

I should also declare that the nest-egg that my wife and I have assembled to see us through our sunset years was largely put together while I manoeuvred Burger King Corporation through its own particular brand of white water – so I owe the industry a lot.

I am, however, going to ask you to ignore both the above qualifications, and bear with me while I let fly. This Sad Bastard is dead wrong.

His, and we assume the Church's, attack bemoans the death of the collective meal, which has been one of history's binding agents for the family. The traditional family model – with its associated behaviour, activities and attitudes – has all but gone, and I DO share the sadness at its passing. In my formative years – say from age five through to my early teens – it was a rare day when my mother, father, sister and I didn't assemble around the table for at least one meal. These occasions had a huge impact on the kind of family we were and the kind of guy I became, and the fact that they have largely disappeared from all family lives is a loss to the values and style of the whole planet.

To put a big chunk of the blame on their disappearance on the emergence of fast food, however, is fatuous. The biggest single element in the deconstruction of the family came when mom stopped shouting: 'C'mon all you guys, dinner's ready. Come and get it' and moved to 'Hey guys, whaddya want to eat? Can I ding something in the microwave for you? Or will you ding your own? Then you can eat it while phoning your friends, or in your own room, and somebody else will clean up afterwards. If you don't want that, here's some cash and you can get something after the movies.'

I look forward to a Catholic edict on the effects of THIS change of behaviour on the family, and, while we are at it, on the presence of TVs in kid's bedrooms, personal stereos, working mums and mobile phones.

The age we live in has thrown massive change at all of us. Some phenomenally good, but most of that is accompanied by stuff we can't handle. Unprecedented wealth creation has benefited millions – but it has been divisive, with the gap between rich and poor widening. There are still too many poor people in rich countries and too many rich people in poor ones. The Information Age has revolutionized every aspect of accessing data and communication – but opened cyberspace to terrorists and paedophiles. These are the uncomfortable by-products of progress, as is the demise of the 'traditional' family.

But I am sick of the fast food world taking hits from shallow thinkers who can't see beyond the end of their quills. Everybody has a go – we are air-dirtiers, carcinogen-generators, body-fat developers and, now, it seems, family-destroyers. Let me give the detractors some fast food for thought.

If you go into a McDonald's in any shopping mall on a Saturday, at lunchtime, you will see families eating together. Some of them (I grant you not all of them) happily smiling and chatting amongst themselves. If you examine the WHOLE zip code that contains that mall, during the same lunch hour, you will not find a single family together at a domestic table. Trust me. Ironically, fast food outlets, which are cheap to visit and provide a range of food for the whole family, are now among the few remaining *enablers* that glue a family together around a dining table.

When I was CEO of Burger King, I used to get millions of figures shovelled in front of me. One stuck in my mind then, and is still with me today. We sold two million Whoppers *every day* across the world. That's two million people – about 0.35% of the earth's TOTAL population – who got at least one cheap, hot, substantial, nourishing meal in every 24-hour period. And here's another aspect that these gloomy plonkers find hard to handle – most of these two million who opt for the Whopper, or whatever else it might be from the huge range of quick-service food available, do so because they prefer it to what else is on offer.

Is quick-serve food destroying the health of the civilized world? This probably annoys me most of all. Of course, if you eat three large pizzas a day, 7 days a week for 30 years, you will explode, Monty Python-style, and discolour several nearby walls. Ditto hamburgers, fried chicken, burritos and anything else – quick, slow or self-service. But fast food restaurants are not the problem here – personal weakness and/or addiction and/or greed are the problems. It becomes a matter of how you use the fast food joints and how you eat.

I love Julia Child. She talks more common sense than any hundred of the current TV chef-entertainers. Listen to what she says about how to eat:

> *Small helpings; no seconds; no snacking; a little bit of everything and have a good time.*

It is my observation (although sadly not my personal experience) that if you applied such glorious commonsense to ANY way of eating, you would be perfectly healthy. If you applied it to a life and a diet that had to be, or was by choice, predominantly in fast food restaurants, you would be just fine.

Not all of the modern way of eating is defensible, however. Now, if His Holiness in the Vatican had loosened his gown and taken a shot at the American practice of putting *cheese in a can*, he would have found me lined up right behind him.

HELLO AOL, GOODBYE OLDSMOBILE

As if the day wasn't bad enough. Just as I am facing the thought of a quarter century having passed without Elvis, my batman wakes me early to tell me some breathtaking news. The first mega-selling record of the new millennium has hit the charts, and it is selling at a rate that means it may not be beaten for another thousand years.

I cannot believe it when he tells me the name of the successful artists. It is the Beatles. A band that broke up 30 years ago, with two of them now dead. One of the survivors, Ringo, wasn't even the best drummer *in the group*. They are, however, selling a copy of their new compilation album every six seconds. It contains all their No.1 hits from their Golden Age. As they have not done anything new for three decades, this has ceased to be about performing and become all about branding.

We should use the Beatles, I decide, to expand our knowledge of what has happened to two other brands – one a fiery comet, the other in a hospice.

The fiery comet is America Online. Half a decade ago, not many consumers had heard of it, and to those who had it was one of an emerging group of Internet Service Providers. All of them were fighting for the attention of the rapidly increasing population of Internet users. If anything, AOL was handicapped by not being a mainstream operating system provider (as were, for example, Microsoft and Apple) so it had to convince users to choose it and then load it into our computers ourselves.

Today, even after having its market capitalization savaged as a result of the tech-stock meltdown and its stupidly advised merge with Time Warner, it is one of the world's most recognized brands. Measure it how you will, it is a Beatles-style ascendancy. Remember, it went from soup to nuts in just over a decade.

Let's look at this story and register two things. First, in today's global village, the rewards for success almost defy belief in their potential to arrive at speed and with mind-blowing magnitude. Apart from the planet, and the ability of a machine to type zeros, there are no limits. If you invent something and develop it in a remote island off Scotland, and it works for people in Taiwan, you can rest assured the wherewithal exists today to get supply meeting demand in a heartbeat. If you doubt that, just think about Nokia and a place called Finland – now one of the world's top five most recognized brands.

The second aspect of AOL's take-off that fascinates me is that I don't think its success is about better technology. Of course, great technology is present, but the reasons why I originally chose it, along, I believe, with about 30 million others, are not because I weighed the technical specifications of one server against another. Jesus, no. I chose it because it did two things that winning brands, both high-tech and low-tech, have been doing forever. It made itself *distinct* in a cluttered and competitive market by being the first of the

Big ISPs to offer a set fee structure for unlimited use. Effectively, AOL bet the ranch on this move, and it was against the collective financial and technical wisdom of the time. It nearly broke them technically and financially. But it changed the market, and from then on AOL led it.

The second thing it did, and I believe this to be Steve Case's real genius, was to use high technology to present the service to the consumer in a low-technology way. It's called *knowing your customer.* He did, better than anybody.

I'm aware there are few business writers today who will be listing AOL in the 'win column'. The meltdown of the combined Time Warner/AOL stock price since the merge has left many commentators picking fly shit out of the pepper of what they see as a wreckage. And, I admit, had I been carrying their stock, I wouldn't be too happy. There is a bigger picture here, however, and at the core of AOL there remains a powerful and distinctive brand. Let's remember, not only the brand but *the industry* they are in didn't really *exist* but a decade ago. The industry they are in is still in its *infancy.* They have plenty of time, skill and opportunity to soar again.

In parallel with the rise of AOL, we witnessed the sun setting on an iconic American brand. General Motors is phasing out Oldsmobile. I caught the press announcement on US TV, and it was – rather sadly I thought – given by bright young man, full of energy, who looked as though he had a promising future somewhere else. His presence made the occasion rather poignant. When I thought of the once mighty Oldsmobile, I couldn't get a picture of Fat Elvis out of my mind.

Is there a finite life span for brands? Is there an equivalent of our human threescore years and ten? Is there a statistical average life expectancy, which some brands don't reach and some over-reach, but NONE of them can defy indefinitely?

It was Chou en Lai who, when asked his view on the impact of the French Revolution some two centuries earlier, remarked that it was probably too soon to tell. The same reflection may apply to this question. A few brands like Coca-Cola, Guinness, Quaker, Heinz and Campbell's are now older than the eldest human, and show no sign of needing corporate euthanasia – so we may need to wait to do a statistical analysis. In the meantime, you'll have to make do with my theory – which is that *immortality can happen*. The Grim Reaper can be beaten.

It is a view I formed out of failure. In the mid 1980s I was made head of a company that included the tired British steak house chain called Berni. We tried everything to reinvent it – but in the end gave up and sold it. It was in the middle of Thatcher's Fuck-You Age, and nobody wanted to be hauled back in time to when you saved up for a month or two to go out for a cheap meal. In its heyday, you would be confronted by a choice of two starters, a range of four or five plated main courses, and a *gourmet* finish of apple pie with ice cream or some shagged out cheese 'n' biscuits. We tried everything, but it seemed to have just too much baggage and seemed to have lost its relevance to a British public with rapidly changing tastes.

I spent a lot of time thinking about this brand, and I confess my early thesis was that it was a simple case of a good, honourable life coming to an inevitable death, as I assumed all brands must. It was only with (much) deeper reflection that I realized it need not have died. Our problem was we tried to reinvent it *too late*. Not only had the brand peaked, but it was declining fast – and that throws up a set of circumstances in which it is almost impossible to reinvent.

The most effective reinventions are done BEFORE the rot sets in, while sales are still *growing*. A good test is that, when you announce the radical changes you are proposing, people look at you as though you are mad. There are loud cries of 'don't fix it, it ain't broke', which you have to ignore. Those who have got vested interests in the brand – investors, employees, suppliers and some customers – won't like what you are proposing because they think it's too early and too risky. You must not weaken – and if you need help I suggest you write OLDSMOBILE in large letters on a piece of paper and stick it on your desktop. Change before the brand baggage is picked up and before relevance is gone forever.

It can be done. Just look at Madonna. Look at Burberry.

It takes real bravery. Nobody likes changing a winner, but if you have the courage to do it, the rewards can be – literally – immortality.

I started this bit on branding with the Beatles. I'll finish it with Elton John. I just happen to have seen him performing on the TV. I should tell you that he holds a special place in the lives of our family. When we were driving to get our eldest son christened we were still short of a middle name for him. Elton came on the car radio and sang *Daniel*. That was all we needed. Elton is, however, also now well into his Fat Elvis period. I think the young man from Oldsmobile could and should now help him with his next career move.

DR WHO?

This week I am starting with a quiz. Early in the new millennium, at the head of the massive Bridgestone Corporation, the Japanese conglomerate that owns the Bridgestone Firestone US-based tyre manufacturing subsidiary, was a shadowy man. He happened to be Japanese, but that is irrelevant. My question has a breathtaking simplicity: *what was his name?*

As soon as I wrote that, I realized it was unfair to a section of my audience. Americans can't handle a question like that, so for my US audience, I need to give you an option from multiple choices. So, which of the following was he?

a)   Mr Sushi Sashimi
b)   Mr Sony Anaconda

c) Dr No

d) Mr Midrange Yamaha

You may phone a friend.

Unfortunately, like you, I do not know the answer, and therein lies the problem. Everybody who has owned a TV, radio or had access to any media during the first years of the new millennium, should, by now, know this guy's name. He should be like a member of the family.

Apparently, one person in twenty of all those who have ever been born is alive today. It would seem that a healthy proportion of them have Ford Explorers, an enormously popular, if gas-guzzling, sports utility vehicle. These are largely driven by women who then need a bottle of Evian to see them through the physical rigours of an afternoon hopping from the mall to picking up the kids from school.

In the US, most of the Explorers had Firestone tyres on them. These tyres became the subject of the new millennium's first great consumer goods disaster – and it was a doozie. Millions of them were recalled and, in the age-old American way, the courts will take years to now decide liability and compensation, and another herd of attorneys will get soaked in gold. Many of the accusations include fatalities resulting from car crashes resulting from tyre failures.

In the world of product recalls, this is a Big Deal. It threatens to hole the massive Bridgestone Firestone Corporation below the water line. Even given the best possible set of future events for the company, it will be years before it recovers. If you hold shares in the company, they are not likely to be among the jewels in your portfolio. The company had massive adverse publicity. The situation cried out for a leader to stand up and take control of the boat. We needed a speech from somebody from the very top of the company who looks us in the eye and says:

This is what's happened, this is what's happening, this is what
we're doing and this is what we stand for as a company – in good
times and bad.

The basic new millennium operations manual for How To Behave
in these circumstances came from an unlikely source. When the
World Trade Centre got smashed, the powers that be decided that
the nation's elected leader, George W. Bush, should go into hiding.
It was left to the mayor of New York, Rudy Giuliani, who happened
to be coming to the end of a once-great but rapidly declining term of
office, to stick his head above the trench. He was visible *everywhere,*
seeing and being seen. His initial speech ('This is what I know, this is
what I don't know') rang out like a bell. There was to be no bullshit,
no hiding. Whatever the truth was, however unpleasant, that – and
that alone – is what we would deal in.

Contrast that to the tyre guy when his company faced an equivalent level of corporate disaster. He chose the Bush Way of Leadership – hidden away somewhere until the dust clears and the PR and
security guys say it's safe to come out and lead again. I don't know
about you, but I still don't know the guy's name (the Japanese guy,
not Bush). Nor do I know what he looks like.

It begs another question: just what is the role and responsibility
of modern mega-corporate leadership?

I read the other day (don't ask – some magazine on a plane
– I've forgotten) that the current crop of corporate *Grandes Fromages*
may be the last. Today's global corporations are just TOO big and
TOO complicated for one person to encompass all that is needed
to provide added-value control and direction. The range of skills
required from now on will be beyond that of even the Gates, Eisn-
ers, Welches and O'Reillys of the generation shortly heading for the
nursing home.

I agree, but only to a point. I believe leadership of a different
definition will emerge. Its role will still be crucial to the success of
the enterprise.

It is my observation that the leader's job will be to dream the dream. These folk see shapes in the future that ordinary mortals do not see. In post-war Italy, Luciano Benetton saw a vision of fashion retailing that was completely alien to his time. Bill Gates saw a PC on every table. The leader will still see those crazy pictures and will still convince the cynical to follow the dream. But after that he or (increasingly, I'm delighted to report) she will need to back off a bit. What you do to deliver the dream needs to be left to good people brought in with specialist skills – who are left to get on with it. And the leader's job moves from WHAT the corporation does to HOW it goes about it.

I believe that HOW a company goes about its business is now becoming one of the key differentiators in cluttered, competitive markets. And I don't just mean conventional consumer markets – I include the ultra-competitive employment and investment markets as well.

It's about HOW responsive – how sensitive – a company is to consumers, investors, employees, vendors, distributors, communities and the environment. It's about what it stands for. It defines the company personality. Making decisions on these, and constantly reinforcing them publicly, will become a constant and crucial element of modern corporate leadership.

Linked with that role is the management of what I call 'corporate optics'. These are the signals the company gives off to its assorted audiences. It is partly science, partly art. It is partly proactive, partly reactive. It is a fundamental of modern leadership, and *never more so than in times of disaster*. Most corporate audiences, including consumers, will – given time – forgive an honest mistake. But broken trust and lost respect take seed like malignant tumours. If you are perceived to be hiding, you are perceived to be hiding something. It is not the time to push lawyers and junior management on stage.

On current form, there is a possibility that my great, great, great grandchildren will come round and consider buying Firestone tyres. Dr No (I lied to you, the answer was 'c' in the quiz above) could change that and bring it forward at least 100 years. But unless he, personally, looks me straight in the eye, via the world's media, and tells me this is what he knows, and this is what he doesn't know, and both are self-evidently true, I am a lost cause for his products.

ONLY WHEN I LAUGH

My word, I feel healthy. My hair is shining, my eyes are clear and my skin has an alabaster sheen to it. My body fat percentage has plummeted into the low seventies, and my blood pressure no longer sets off garage-door remote controls. When I step out of the shower, and look guardedly at the full-length mirror, I am no longer reminded of a teapot. I look and I think about Buns Of Steel.

I put all this good news down to laughter.

In the US, a study by the University of Maryland Medical Center, Baltimore, found, in summary, that people who laugh a lot are healthier. Laughter may even reduce the dreaded threat of cardiac problems.

Laughter just has to be the cause of the new Healthy Me. I keep looking at the business pages and hooting with the stuff. I don't need

George Carlin or a sitcom, just give me the *Wall Street Journal* or the *Financial Times*, and I'm a lost cause for the morning.

It started a while back. Kirk Kerkorian got miffed at Jurgen E. Schrempp of DaimlerChrysler. The 'merger of equals' between the two motor giants apparently hasn't turned out that way. DC does, of course, contain a squillion dollars of Mr Kerkorian's money as an investment, and when he invests, *he invests*. He wants to be on the inside track for everything. Annoyingly for Captain Kirk, and hilariously for the rest of us, Jurgen let it slip that *it was never actually planned to be a merger of equals at all*. That was just a ruse to get the deal done.

If there was any doubt, readers of my extensive journalism had their eyes opened when the announcement was made a few years ago. You read it here first. Goliath rolled over David. Ten minutes of due diligence conducted from Mars would have made that clear to anybody.

Chrysler has now found its place in the DC Empire. It will, I believe, eventually be run part-time by an 18-year-old German, based in Germany, earning the equivalent of $6.50 an hour. In fairness, he will visit Detroit every second year. Organizationally, this important position will report to the DC Vice-President of Lost Causes (along with some of Jurgen's other 'Mergers of Equals' in Mitsubishi and Hyundai). So, Kirk's loaded up for a legal bear hunt. Just what the investors and company need now. Yeah, right.

I'd hardly wiped the tears away from this lot, when, around the same time, I read that the Coca-Cola Board whipped the rug from under new boss Douglas Daft's plan to buy Quaker (well, Gatorade …). But these guys, led by Warren 'Jimmy' Buffet, another 'low profile' investor, didn't quietly throw an early fire blanket on Douglas' plan to give up 10% of Coke's equity as a price for the new brands. They waited until he was right at the end of his air supply, with the deal finalized and the champagne on ice; with the interviews lined up and the world's press alerted; with PR folk ready to roll and with the Quaker board waiting at the end of the phone. THEN they harpooned Douglas. Quite near the groin.

Laugh? I thought I'd never stop. Now, tell me – who is going to deal substantively with Dafty again? Would you? Or would you tell him you'd sooner deal directly with his daddy?

If THAT wasn't enough, it was also around the same time that the UK's troubled blue chip retailer, Marks & Spencer, announced that – as part of their Big Turnaround Plan, which also involved combining the Chairman and CEO role into one and giving it to a Mr Luc Vandevelde, whose name alone would score 150 at Scrabble – they would ADVERTISE. This was an unprecedented step for what was then an arrogant has-been brand. We waited, in suspense, for the first showing.

When it came, and when we saw it, it was hard to limit oneself to a belly laugh. This was the stuff of Jim Carrey. Apparently, their advertising agency convinced the M&S *Grandes Fromages* that women, when they buy clothes, don't want to look like Buffy the Vampire Slayer – they want to look like, er, er, *themselves*. Accordingly (and the more sensitive of you may want to shield your eyes here) we were treated to a, well … a big … woman, running, naked (but very romantically and discreetly facing away from the camera), into a hazy sunset (or sunrise – it was difficult to tell).

Now, British pension fund managers are not known for a) their sense of humour and b) their political correctness, and you must understand that I am only quoting the next bit (exactly) in the interests of accuracy. When interviewed in the financial press, this beleaguered major investor, running his fingers metaphorically through the ruins of his pension fund's huge holding in M&S, uttered the immortal words:

> They've still got a chance, but for Christ's sake they've got to get that fat bird off the telly.

I apologize for hitting you straight between the eyes with that, and recognize it may offend. But it was printed. I'll not tell you what newspaper it was in, but it wasn't on white paper.

In fairness, he was right. They did have a chance. They did ditch the ad campaign – and employed a new CEO who seemed to know what he was doing. As I write, the comeback is gathering momentum – but memories of the Fat Bird still linger and make my stomach ache. My eyes were sore from crying.

Then I read that the average Internet stock – and that's taking them all into account – is trading at less that 5% of its historic high. There are more stock options under more water than you could shake a stick at.

Then, just when you think you can't laugh anymore, Martha Stewart takes a bath in the USA. On the back of rumoured insider trading, the squeaky clean ice-maiden Diva-Bore drags the market valuation of her empire down by more than half.

Unashamedly I repeat Oscar Wilde's quote: 'You'd have to have a heart of stone not to laugh.'

MORE STUFF, LESS CHOICE

We are, it seems, stuffed with stuff. That's a line I stole from the best business book I have read in years, Naomi Klein's *No Logo* (Harper-Collins 2000). It's about 100 pages too long, but it is a readable piece of scholarship documenting the insidious take over of the planet by a double-handful of super brands.

Stuffed with stuff. As I reflect on my own modern life, and that of our children (now grown up), and the generation following them, it seems a wonderfully apposite way of describing our stuff-laden lives. Today, I have possessions to a degree I would not have thought possible when I left my austere childhood. I have heard it said that 75% of the acquisitions made by adult males are made for the effect they will have on other people. My only observation on that, which is based on personal and noted experience, is that such a figure is 24% too low. But I do have a groovy car.

There is, however, a paradox. As the availability of stuff rises, along with our propensity and capability to acquire it, it is my belief that the actual *choices* available to us are diminishing.

Stuff usually comes from shops, which may now of course be virtual. They may only exist in cyberspace, or a catalogue, or on the TV screen. They increasingly line up in a shopping mall. Choices, choices, choices? I think not.

A long time ago, when I couldn't afford to buy stuff, ironically I lived in a town where the high street had a vast variety of retailers offering it to me. All these retailers were individual, all doing their own thing. If you went to the next town there was another lot – with few, if any, repeats. They had their own stores, reflecting their individuality and their town's local products and character. Now, there are only a handful of high streets. I have to go to the mall. Scarily, the new mall extension in Milton Keynes in England looks exactly like Dadeland Mall in Miami, with Starbucks, Gap, McDonald's, Virgin (*et al.* – you know them well) the only people who can make sense of the rents. In cyberspace, it's the same names with the same stuff.

If I want to catch up on the daily news, mega-mergers and deregulation mean that it is tough to find a media vehicle that is independent. In the UK, if Rupert Murdoch, the head of the worldwide multimedia empire, lost his temper one day and in a fit of Mike Tyson-like behaviour, bit off part of one of Prince Charles's ears (a good idea, by the way), could we rely on his assorted newspapers and his Sky television to give objective coverage? Or his media interests in the US and the rest of the world? Could ABC television report objectively if Michael Eisner of Disney eloped with one of the 101 Dalmatians – when both companies are part of the same conglomerate? CNN, my favourite worldwide news source, was owned by Time Warner. How objectively can they now track the progress (or otherwise) of the massive merge between that company and AOL which produced their new owners?

This goes way beyond news media. If I go into Blockbuster to rent a video, do I get the best critical or box office choices – or am I pushed towards their sister company's in-house movie productions? Is the record being promoted with a huge display in a Virgin store being pushed on its merits or because it's on the Virgin record label?

If I want to fly out of an airport, it is true that the destinations available to me are diverse and growing in number. But if the airport in question has become a 'hub' for one of the decreasing number of big carriers, what choice of route, carrier and price do I have? If I use that airport and carrier regularly, I get further glued in by superbly effective (for the carrier) loyalty programs.

I happen to like Cole Haan shoes. This fact alone should convince the doubters of the statistic quoted in the second paragraph of this essay. Nonetheless, no trip to New York is complete for me without popping in the CH shop, and trying to convince myself that $250 is good value for a pair of shoes because they will last and I will get good use out of them (blah blah blah). Conversely, I happen to dislike Nike. It's not a big deal, and not pointed at any product line. It doesn't keep me awake at night. I guess it's just a bit of a nonconformist rebel in me coming out 40 years too late. In my eyes Nike CEO and rock-star wannabe Phil Knight looks a complete Tosser in those wrap-around sunglasses. I don't like what they have done to my beloved sport of soccer, and I don't like their smash-mouth brand arrogance.

Now then, it turns out Nike own Cole Haan. So now what do I do?

The Big cola guys and the Big fast food brands are driving for (a.k.a. paying for) 'exclusive' representation at colleges and schools. Last time I looked, exclusive means, well, exclusive. In other words, choices are removed. It doesn't matter whether the students like it or not. It doesn't matter whether it's *good* for the students or not. Education is a business now, and has to be commercially creative in sourcing funds.

It can get quite scary. The mega-retailers are increasingly using their leverage not just to control the range, but *the content* of some of the products they 'allow' us to buy. If the cover of a CD isn't completely nipple-free, or some song lyrics are not in line with White Anglo Saxon Protestant (WASP) creeds, the message back to the record label is that it's the mega-retailer's way or the highway. Few labels (or artists) choose the highway. Vanishing cream is rubbed on the offending nipple and the naughty words are lost in a remix. Now, just suppose the buying unit of one of these mega-retailers was based in, oh let's just make this up – one of the 'deep southern' States in the US – ain't it jus' *real* comforting to know that some good ole southern US of A bozo, probably with the same DNA as his cousins, and who almost certainly owns a gun, is protecting the values of the civilized world? Yeah, right. Although I haven't researched it extensively, to my knowledge nobody has yet died from exposure to the sight of a nipple.

More stuff, *less choice*. More liberty, *less freedom*. Welcome to the new millennium.

Now, if you will excuse me, I am off to incinerate my new shoes.

REMEDIES FOR THE 'OHNO MOMENT'

I have just had, unquestionably, THE business idea of the new millennium. It will make money in a way that makes Microsoft look like Amazon.com.

Most of the research has been done, so venture capital needs will be small. The only snag on the radar screen is that I will need some basic knowledge of chemistry for the final stages of product development, and when I last sat examinations in that subject in, I think, 1962, I achieved less than stellar marks. In fact, I do believe I went through my final year in that subject, at the age of 16, without once achieving a percentage mark in an exam that exceeded the average annual pay rise for nurses. But if someone can help me with chemistry, we are home and dry.

The 'morning-after' pill, Levonelle by brand name, abortifa-
cient in its properties, is now available in the UK on a non prescrip-
tion, over-the-counter basis. An effective dosage of two pills costs
about £20, and purchasers need only have that money and be 16
years old. They will also, of course, need to have recently been involved in a Legover Situation.

In my understanding, the pill definitely does two physical
things and may do a psychological third. It definitely removes
the physical consequences of a previous decision, and it definitely
restores the physical status quo. It may also convince the person
involved that what actually happened didn't actually happen – perhaps the greatest feat of all.

Now, I'm not goofy enough to get into a public debate on the
religious, social and political ramifications of putting such a product
on open sale. My plan – and, if I may say so, my genius – will be to
make and market one of these pills *for business*. My working brand
name will be *Gibbonelle*. I plan to charge much more than £20 a hit.
Much, much more.

I can hear your coffee cups splatter on the floor. Why the hell
didn't you think of it first? Too late, I have patented it. You take two
of my little blue pills the day after making a dumb business decision, and you effectively rub vanishing cream on it. It will be worth
zillions.

Why am I so confident in its money-making potential? I have
been in and around Big Business for more than 30 years, and I know
that I, alone – never mind the prats who have recently lead Daimler-
Chrysler, WorldCom, British Airways, Enron and Marconi (to name
but five) – would have coughed up half a year's salary to undo some
decisions that seemed oh-so-robust during the day before. In the
cold, sober light of the morning after, they looked like the dumbest
things ever.

There is nothing quite like the moment you realize something
has gone royally wrong. It is, truly, a horrible feeling. It's called the

'Ohno moment'. Your stomach feels like you've swallowed a sumo wrestler's jock strap.

Towards the end of my corporate career, during which I had built a solid reputation for picking good people and assembling good teams, I had the luxury – the ridiculous luxury – of working with somebody for a year before I confirmed him in a senior position. Yes, it was a 'he' – so the ladies can now sit back, in anticipation, and enjoy this. I used every minute of the year to make up my mind about him. Finally, he was appointed, a decision I made with absolute confidence. About ten minutes later I looked at him with what must have been different eyes, and, to my initial self-disbelief, realized I had made a massive misjudgement. Ohno. Ohnonono. Not by anybody else's standards, I hasten to add, but by my own. Oh, for a morning-after pill.

How much do you think Roberto Goizuetta, the late and (much) lamented head of Coca-Cola, would have paid for two morning-after pills that would have aborted the launch of New Coke? Can you imagine what a Fun-O room that must have been at the final imperious moment when they realized that they had got THAT wrong? I met Mr Goizuetta a couple of times during my stint on the bridge of the good ship Burger King, and I would NOT have wanted to be the guy who told him.

The business market will be infinite – but my pills will have potential use in other walks of life. What would President Bush (the old thicko-one, not the new thicko-one) have given on that special morning, a few years back, for a pill that would have removed from the world's TV screens the spectacular images of him up-chucking all over the trousers of the Japanese Prime Minister the night before?

I could market a set of pills directly to my beloved Manchester City soccer team. Despite their current (albeit short) run of success, I am assuming, of course, that they will carry on the habits of the last 30 years and get every decision on playing staff hopelessly wrong. They can take one look at all the guys they acquire when they turn up for training the morning after, then they just take two pills and – *voilà* – they've gone back to Leeds' reserves.

Clearly, these pills will bring back risk-taking into business. Businesses will no longer be afraid to make mistakes. CEOs all over the world, with two of my pills in the top right-hand drawers of their desks, will sign off risky new investments, product launches and new market expansions. Within five years every corporate lawyer will have been sacked. *There are simply no downsides to my scheme.*

The least I expect for delivering this breakthrough to the world is a knighthood and, in mild pursuit of this cause, I have sent a complimentary pair of pills to Her Majesty to pass on to Prince Charles. That may not be enough for him, of course.

I fear I may have told you too much for my own good. Those with more energy, resources and skill than me will hear of this and try and get a piece of the action. You are welcome to try, but be prepared to duke it out in the courts.

Frankly – to give you some hope – it might turn out to be too big for me to handle on my own in the medium and long term. Without any marketing or PR, I already have my first order for two pills from Hugh Grant. He's visiting LA again soon, and wants to be prepared.

THE LAST POST
(OFFICE)

I am, it seems, almost constantly in the air over the Atlantic these days, flitting like a demented hummingbird between the US and UK. American Airlines kindly recorded my prowess as a latter-day Columbus by writing to me to tell me I had completed an aggregate of three million air miles with them, which entitled me to a silver sex-aid (which they sent enclosed in a handsome box), and elevation from Executive Platinum to Papal Titanium class for my frequent flyer activity. This means I call them up and tell them when I'm ready to go.

Actually, on closer examination, it wasn't a silver sex aid, but rather a whatsit-thingummy for sealing half empty wine bottles. Hey, I'm from Europe. I've never opened a bottle I didn't finish, so this took a bit of working out.

The trans-Atlantic journeying continues to highlight the differences and similarities between our two nations. It is true we are still divided by a common language, but that divide is narrowing as we're all drifting into some slangy modern version of English. Some of the traditional language quirks look like they will stay forever – Americans do still pronounce tomato as tom-ay-to, but we Brits don't. That's because we can't afford them anymore.

On balance, however, more and more is linking us. One example of a new togetherness is through our two hopelessly myopic postal services.

Occasionally this writer is moved to award the Kerosene Oil Trophy to businesses where short-sightedness has not only damaged the short-term outlook, but threatened long-term survival. The trophy itself is a tribute to the greatest management thesis ever written – Theodore Levitt's 'Marketing Myopia', written for HBS[1] in the early 1960s.

At the end of the nineteenth century, kerosene had a virtual monopoly as a fuel for lighting. Levitt's thesis, if you remember (I'm flattering you – you have NO idea, have you?) was that the kerosene industry died because it thought it was in the kerosene industry. It wasn't, of course. It was actually in the *illumination* industry, and when cheaper, cleaner methods of illumination came along with gas and electricity, the kerosene oil guys called for the equivalent of Dr Kervorkian, our beloved assisted-suicide expert. The point being that IF they had recognized they were in the illumination industry, they would have THEMSELVES developed gas and electricity. Terminal myopia.

Now turn that thinking to the postal services industry in both the UK and US. By limiting itself to postal services and some ancillary bits and pieces, both these have missed out on the explosion

---

1 Harvard Business School. I am all for short cuts and 'micro-waveable' learning – so buy yourselves HBS' 15 Business Classics. It's got all you'll ever need.

of non postal communications in the last two decades.[2] Not only is that a huge business development opportunity missed, it will be an omission that will, in time, threaten the existence of both services as we know them today.

There have been two developments in the last 20 years that they have missed out on. The first was the development of facsimile document transmission. I am old enough to remember an odd machine first appearing in the cutting-edge companies, and then an explosion as technology improved and prices fell. As ever, private consumer use lagged behind business, but then they started appearing in homes. The post offices of both nations could and SHOULD have seen this coming, and invested in the development of the industry and set them selves up as Community Fax Centres. Instead they waved it through – and to this day can only watch as the world's massive fax business goes on without them having the tiniest piece of it.

If that was kerosene thinking *par excellence,* their approach to the Internet has been spectacularly myopic. I am quite clear in my view that the fact that the dominant server in the US is called AOL, and not USPSOL,[3] is a life-threatening mistake for the latter. In the UK, we would have been accessing the Internet via something called GPOonline[4] for the last five years if anybody in power there could have seen beyond the end of their nose.

The future of the traditional postal services – dispatching and delivering envelopes and packages – is not all bleak, despite the fact that conventional letter writing will probably be all over within two decades. You could argue that as e-trade eats in to the traditional retail market, the demand for package distribution will increase as people buy their stuff online and have it delivered. In addition,

---

2 It is hard to believe but there was really no widely available Internet as recently as the early 1990s. And Bed Linen was something you slept in – way before he became a terrorist.
3 United States Postal Services On-line. Which doesn't exist. Which is my point.
4 General Post Office On-line. Ditto.

direct-to-consumer marketing programs – junk mail, catalogues, and personalized 'offers' arriving in your mailbox etc. – will also increase. But both these will be of scant consolation for the missed opportunity for these two businesses to have waved through the Internet when they were in pole position to be at the forefront of it.

They will also have to fight as never before for the declining traditional postal business, and the new potential markets, as de-regulation and non traditional competition bites them high on the inner thigh.

I do not forecast a bright future for either of them, and do not believe they will exist in their current forms a decade from now. Facile and superficial name changes such as the UK Post Office's corporate 'rebranding' as *Consignia*, and then rebranding back again, merely emphasize the point. It's all a dollar short and a day late.

Marketing myopia is simply poor long-range vision. Nike realized early on that they were not in the sports shoe or clothes market – they were in the Hunt for Cool industry. Häagen-Dazs is really in the market for the small self indulgency. Fancy fountain pens are not in the pen market – they are in the corporate gift market. Starbucks is in a market called the 'Third Place' (i.e. somewhere to meet which is not the home or work).

It's easy when you know how, and hindsight in these cases has crystal-clear 20/20 vision. But when you get it wrong it can be terminal. And I know. I've seen Sly Stallone's recent movies.

THE BENEFITS OF S.E.A.L.

What happens in America usually takes two or three years to reach England. As a Brit, it was, therefore, with a feeling of horror that I saw my first, US-style, stretch limo over here. It was one of those that, if you half close your eyes, look like a cruise liner. They also have the same manoeuvrability in tight spaces. It was parked, of all places, in front of a 400-year-old village pub, and looked like a cold sore on upper lip of a pretty face.

The stretch limo is universally associated with Hollywood, rap singers bearing arms (as provided for in the US Constitution) and the trappings of corporate power in the US.

I need to start this essay by revealing my views on them. Yes, I confess I have been inside several, but my position is that I would not willingly go in one today even if it offered me the only escape route from a black mamba crawling up the inside of my trouser leg.

A decade ago, as a newly appointed – and imported – CEO of Burger King, I inherited a wonderful assistant. She was (and still is) a 'can-do/take-charge' lady. She assumed that the new boss would be the same as the old boss, and booked me a limo to pick me up as I arrived at Orlando airport on an early head-hunting mission. Knowing no different, I got in the thing. The driver, who was just about within earshot, then proceeded to start the engine and drive *about a hundred yards* to the hotel where the meeting was scheduled. I could have got in the back, walked down the car and got out of the driver's door and had my meeting. I banned them for all corporate use.

A couple of years later we booked 'Stormin' Norman Schwartz-kopf to speak at our annual (Burger King) convention – his first such event since leaving the US army after the Gulf War. This was a real popular guy in the US at the time. Even though he had left the army, the folks back in Washington remained concerned for his safety, and took precautions everywhere he went in public. As we were all on standby to receive the great man at convention, a bunch of secret service guys were hanging about, their eyes never still. These are scary fellas – every one of them bulked up with a bullet-proof vest and clearly carrying a gun or guns. They were not too bothered who knew it either. Some hidden walkie-talkies suddenly crackled. He was arriving. Everybody became alert and tense – and up pulled a HUGE limo outside the hotel reception. The door opened, and there was a moment of eerie stillness. Then out stepped *my tiny wife*.

It transpired that the hotel management, somewhat thankful that we were spending the equivalent of India's GDP on the event, without me or the US government knowing, had sent this doozie of a limo to pick my wife up at the airport. As everybody stared silently at her, Stormin' Norman pulled up behind – *in an old red pick-up truck.*

There and then I formed S.E.A.L. (Senior Executives Against Limos) and I have remained President, Treasurer and the only paid-up member ever since.

It begs the question, of course, as to what is the correct degree of ostentation you should enjoy as a Big Cheese in corporate life. There are negatives to a fully egalitarian approach – I remember one of my corporate managers pleading with me to be a bit more flash when I visited franchisees. His message was that they *expect* ostentation from a corporate leader, that they want their employees and their competitive peers to see that they belong to system of substance, and that they are led by a Big Time Charlie. He was serious and it is a serious point – there are downsides, certainly in a big corporation, to a leader appearing on the scene looking and acting like Bob Geldof.

Another valid point can be made in defence of the indefensible. If you are in the junior ranks of a company, labouring away for 24/7 in an office which is, say, the size of Fatty Arbuckle's coffin, if you don't believe there is a big office and a load of perks at the end of your rainbow, there is not much to keep you turning up and motivated. I mean, what's the point in dicking around on the first rungs of the corporate ladder if you believe that the higher rungs do not bring with them a rosier glow?

Each to his (or her) own. There is, however, a clear trend towards reducing the excesses of corporate style invoked by business leaders, if for no other reason than it can tick off the investment analysts and/or investors and/or pressurized employees by giving off the wrong kind of signals.

I have stopped judging all this by car length or office square footage. There is an appropriate level of *cost* necessary to support the effectiveness and efficiency of each job in a corporation. I believe that cost should be calculated and made public, certainly within the company and to its external shareholders. That's healthy. The defendable can be defended objectively, the indefensible is highlighted for being just that. There is simply no defence for WorldCom *lending*

$400 million to its arsehole of a CEO (Ebbers) who was on the bridge of the ship during its corporate suicide bombing.

In tight, competitive markets, corporate overhead costs are like the fresh water barrel on a fifteenth century galleon crossing the Atlantic. The water has to get everybody there alive. It's finite, and there's not much of it. If one person uses more, another must use less. If it runs out, everybody dies. It calls for judgement.

This approach can actually justify a private jet – but only if it is used like Sam Walton used it. His life was visiting Wal-Marts, day in day out, all over America. He was frugal in the extreme with normal overhead costs, but everybody agreed he added real value visiting stores. A private plane probably doubled or tripled his annual store-visit tally and was money well spent.

On the other hand this approach can't justify a single limo rent if it's only about image and pampering. One of my US bosses was driven in a stretch limo, with only himself for company, from home to work and back every day. It was such an important part of his image that he had a structural wall knocked out in the under-of-fice car park to cater for his big sardine tin. Short of hiring a plane to fly around the town trailing a big banner with 'Look at me, I'm a Wanker' written on it, he couldn't do more to illustrate to the world what he was all about. The annoying thing is he was about much more than that, but both stories tell you all you need to know about right and wrong in this game.

Spend what you *need* to spend to support your job description. No less, no more. That's a ruling that should apply to every job. If you are sending a junior manager to Japan, give them a decent air ticket – one that gives them some room to sleep. If they are important enough to represent you, the cost of getting them there fresh is justified. Conversely, if you are a Big Cheese and you are hopping a short distance – shock everybody and drive yourself – or scrunch up in the back of the plane with the rest of the human race. Your lifestyle is determined by your salary and how you spend it *outside* the business, not corporate perks.

I fear the only way I will stop this unwanted limo invasion in England is to start a scare. So, you will hear it from me first. I am announcing the first outbreak, in the UK, of *mad-limo disease.* Shortly, as is the case, you will read of extensive government programmes to slaughter them all. You can then smile quietly to yourself.

When you have smiled, you can apply to join S.E.A.L.

THE CHANGING FACE
OF GIANTS

I am in Turin, at a convention of European shopping mall developers. They have just realized that the provision of food and drink at such facilities is er ... er ... well, helpful. They do catch on fast.

While in the old city, we grab a look at the famous Shroud (or, at least, a life-sized replica). Everybody has their own theories as to its origin and whether it is fake or real. So have I. I remain convinced it is a prank played by one of the Bee Gees after a heavy 1970s post-concert party in which the lead singer somehow got covered in treacle and fell asleep. The hotel janitor stole his sheets in the morning and the rest is history.

With my limited Italian, I try to read *La Stampa* – the local newspaper. Suddenly I find myself trembling, with a dreadful constriction in my throat. Unless my translation is way off, just over the Alps and across the border in Switzerland, the first McDonald's hotel has opened. One picture tells me everything I can't translate – the headboards on the beds in the double rooms are shaped like Golden Arches. The only restaurant in the hotel is a McDonald's. This is Switzerland, remember. This tiny country has France and Italy as neighbours – nations responsible for two of the planet's great culinary cultures. It gets worse. I think I translate the last sentences of the article correctly: *they are targeting business travellers.*

Is it just me, or is this beyond belief? Should this earth ever require a stereotypical business traveller to send to an inter-planetary convention dealing with the science, it would do well to choose me. I have spent much of my adult life in planes and hotels. I have visited about 50 countries on business. McDonald's are, therefore and by definition, targeting me. So let me tell you what they are up against.

Should I be lucky enough to have a business visit to Switzerland, I would, as is normal, search the web for an hotel. If my web findings indicate that there are 6512 hotel options in the country, a McDonald's hotel would not even be my 6512th choice. No sir. If all the other 6511 were unfortunately full, and the McDonald's was the only one with room at the Inn, I would still book a room in Northern Italy, get up early and *walk across the fucking Alps* to get to my meeting rather than stay in a room with Golden Arches above my bed.

Are they mad? The answer, I suspect, is NO. There are some odd bits and pieces going on in McDonald's which, if you look at them *as a whole*, suggest something quite revolutionary might be going on. It might also be a fast food industry first.

By any measurement McDonald's is one of the world's great brands. The science of branding has changed irrevocably in the last decade, and my observation is that we are seeing the first of the giants recognizing this.

For the last century or so, branding has been about products. Coca-Cola are the classical exponents of this approach – and Mars, Ford and Heinz are but three of many other examples. Branding is about differentiation – distinction – in cluttered and competitive markets. What has changed is how you get that distinction effectively and efficiently. As we noted earlier in this book, much less emphasis is being placed on WHAT you do (the specification and price of your product or service). What's winning and retaining business today is HOW you go about delivering that to the market. What you do still matters of course, but it is the price of entering the game. To win it, you must add style to substance. What you stand for as a business, and the company's 'personality', are both becoming critical differentiators. Branding by reputation, not product, is the name of the new game.

I cannot think of one product that, on its own, could sustain a mighty corporation today, let alone give it a platform to grow. Coca-Cola are leading the way again. Whatever the full reasoning was behind the exit of Douglas Ivester, it would seem that his style as well as his substance played a part. And if you look at Coca-Cola's armoury of drinks products today, many of which are (gasp!) non-carbonated, you will see a very different approach to brand ownership and management evolving. There are now some 1500 products going out under their banner brand name.

Now let's go back to McDonald's. Forever associated with a one-dimensional product and corporate personality, look at what's happening. They bought (and then sold again) a gourmet coffee business called *Aroma*. The product is clearly of interest to them. They have espresso products now in the Swiss Hotel, and they are signalling that they are targeting one of the spiritual homes of espresso coffee – Austria – to develop this potential growth sector. Mc-Caffees (ugh!) are appearing Stateside. They are also duelling with the French, adapting their traditional menu to reflect that when they are in Paris[1] they are not in Wyoming. They have acquired Mexican and rotisserie chicken food service businesses.

---

1 I wish them well. This is a fight I never won in Burger King – the resistance to anything American is such that we looked elsewhere for international prosperity.

Do I see Coke and Macs getting into the dumb stuff of the last two decades and diversifying into film studios? Short answer: NO. But they are changing their faces. They are moving away from single-product dependence – not because those products have no life left in them, but because they are too limiting in personality and growth potential.

Coca-Cola, of course, have gone one step further. I have it very good authority that they actually appointed a guy called Dwayne Brown as Douglas Ivester's successor. Their board, however, being all awash with the new thinking, decided (after reading one of my theses) that such a name would never do for the dawn of the New Era. So, they gave the designate appointee a short list of names *to choose from if he wanted the job*. It appears he chose 'Douglas Daft'.

Makes you wonder about the rest of the list.

NO WONDER WE ARE
LIVING LONGER

I am floating on the Mediterranean, face up, feet towards France. I am determined to do two things, both of which require superhuman determination. First, I will keep my toes above water until further notice. Second, I will write this column (in principle, you understand – even I cannot float with a laptop).

I am inspired by a recent *Provençale* luncheon, which started promptly at 1pm under the olive trees of our rented farmhouse and which finished, in delightful disorganization, around midnight. The efficacy of our dish-washing was not aided by the effects of several beakers of *calvados* that seemed to wink in the starlight.

My theme today will be a short, two-dimensional history of executive dining, culminating in my observations about the correct eating habits for the modern business person.

I say two-dimensional because it will be based on my personal experiences, and they span both a long passage of time, and a business career that hopped from Europe to America. Both dimensions will need careful analysis before any conclusion is drawn.

In my early days, back in England, any executive that could be remotely described as senior would not dream of starting the day's labours without the Full Monty breakfast. Nor would he (and in those days it was about 99% male) contemplate eating this anywhere but in his own (domestic) dining room. Such a breakfast had a number of requirements. First: it would need two butlers, a chef, probably a *sous-chef*, and three kitchen maids and an under-butler for the back stairs. Second: all dishes would be served from under silver tureen lids, lined up on a table by a roaring fire (even in July). Third: there would have to be at least three dishes beginning with 'k' (kippers, kidneys, kedgeree etc.). Several strong, unfiltered cigarettes would be ingested. Work-talk was, of course, forbidden. Phone calls were unheard of. Our man read *The Times*, which had probably been ironed by a fourth butler. Somewhere around 9.30am, fully armed for the trials ahead, he would leave for the train, pecking his wife on the cheek and running through the names of the children again – so that he would have them off pat next time they all shared the same room. He would float into the office in a very agreeable mood. The excitement was such that his blood would be pulsing through the tiny, tiny channels that remained open in his system of veins.

At some stage in the late morning, percolated coffee would be delivered on a silver tray into his office, probably by his assistant's assistant. High-integrity Scottish shortbread biscuits would be served with the coffee, and the break would take place around a meeting with his works manager at a Queen Ann occasional table, positioned exactly fifteen feet and six inches away from his early Edwardian desk.

Luncheon, of course, was the meal for business – and please notice it is *luncheon*, not lunch. This was not a rushed affair, and due process was rigorously observed on a number of fronts. The venue had to be away from prying eyes, preferably a private club where occasional indiscretions were gently rubbed with vanishing cream. It would start around 1pm, and no business was discussed before 4pm. By this time, the last of the pan-fried pigeon breasts had long been digested, and material damage done to a bottle of a) decent claret and b) a crusty (but not ostentatious) port. After all, this was a working day.

Luncheon would then be concluded quickly. A deal would be agreed, and a handshake occurred. *And God help anybody who went back on one of those.*

Luncheon was also the first proving ground of the astonishing mathematical phenomenon: half a bottle of wine is perfect for one, but a full bottle is *not quite enough for two.*

The late afternoon saw the dictation of a letter or two back at the office, with the frugal accompaniment only of hot tea and a selection of small cakes. Cocktails began at 7.30pm promptly, and a curtain came down. The business day had ended. No more business affairs would be aired through that or dinner.

The Big Bang changed it all. That was when London went all high tech and 24/7. The equivalent executive today has a breakfast of wheatgerm extract while running on a treadmill, sending and receiving e-mails on a palm PC, swallowing vitamins and watching his – or her – Bloomberg screen. And it is still only 5am. Said executive may not eat again until late evening, when he or she regroups with a bunch of stressed-out peers around an organic (and team-bonding) vegetarian pizza. Caffeine is forbidden after 11.30am. The mere *idea* of wine with anything would send our hero/heroine into a three-month course of counselling

Somewhere in this transition, I moved to America – and a whole new set of variables was introduced to my confused digestive system. In 1989, having just arrived in the US, I sat opposite a young (male) executive in a New York deli. The time was about 11am – neither one thing nor the other. He ordered a chopped liver sandwich. It arrived, and it was about six inches thick. To my dying day I will never forget the horror of seeing him eating it across the table from me. There are some sights to which an Englishman, frankly, should not be exposed. Slowly, like a reticulated python, he unhinged his lower jaw, and swallowed it whole. *I swear I could see the whole shape of it as it headed down his inner tubes.*

Business eating habits have changed in the US in parallel with Europe, but our analysis of them must factor in two unique-to-Uncle-Sam elements, namely size and speed.

Rule Number One in the US is that *Good equals Big*, and a well-received meal in the US is still one you *can't see over.* To this day, I have nightmares about the amount of food that must have been ordered and left uneaten during my five years with Burger King.

Speed is the other unique factor required of a successful eating experience in the US. In Europe, it can take 100 years to get a garden lawn to its first stage of acceptability. A game of cricket between two countries can take *five days,* during which the players stop for lunch and tea each day. England now boasts an official Slow Food movement. *We like things slow.* To wait 30 minutes for your first course, while you enjoy a winding-down cocktail and eyeball all the other diners, is now a capital offence in some US states. Well, it is in Texas. I mustn't exaggerate.

Sadly, however, today we are all much the same in our executive lives and habits. True, the Italians and French have defended a proper lunch, but most of us have changed with the demands of the times, and most of us are influenced by American-led habits.

Today, my breakfast consists of bran-flakes and skimmed milk. I don't do luncheon – I eat lunch or brunch, and have no alcohol. I still drink WAY too much coffee. Now and again, however, the rebel in me rears up – and I clear the decks for a luncheon that blends the afternoon into the early evening. I get my feet right under the table, and I get tucked in. Sure, I pay for it the morning after, but I can see from here you are all jealous.

And that's not all I can see. My toes have disappeared under water. I must head for land. I stayed afloat for 1277 words. Beat that.

REBEL WITHOUT
A CAUSE

The plan is working all right, but I am paying a personal price.

As you know (and I'd like you to keep it to yourselves as much as possible), for some years now I have enjoyed a not-insubstantial monthly retainer, which has been paid into my Swiss bank account on behalf of at least one of the more notorious Chinese gangs.

The plan is to undermine most, if not all, Western governments and their lackey 'global' brands, so that, when the Great Day arrives, they will have been weakened and capable of less resistance. I have been recording notable success. As I said, however, I am paying a price.

I made my mark on all the recent summit meetings of the Western democracies, and so far I have totted up a broken leg, five broken ribs and pepper-spray burn (Seattle); a cracked skull, one lost eye and nine broken fingers (Gothenburg) and I am still recovering from the bruising and the rubber bullet wounds that the Genoa police handed me this summer. There was also some damage to my liver from the latter escapade, but, in fairness, that might have been due to the 62 *grappas* I had before I took to the streets for my peaceful protest.

I disguised my true cause well, hiding under the umbrella of (at various times) the following 'campaigns': anti-globalism; pro-Kyoto; anti-whaling; anti-salmon farming; anti-genetically modified crops; anti-capital punishment; pro-cannabis legalization; Save The Tiger; Don't Save McDonald's; ban pesticides; Minimum Wage For Nike Slaves; Third World debt relief; Shoot Charlton Heston and Bring Back Abba.

Just what is it these Western leaders don't get? Just because I have a job, money in the bank, a family, two cars, a pension and all the toys I could wish for, can't they understand I am still angry? There is a *fire* burning within me, and I need to throw Molotov cocktails at fascist-pig policemen, and trash buildings to make my point.

Now then, let's you and me stop, and reflect a moment. Does *anybody* know what the hell is going on here? No citizen of a developed nation should fail to understand that there is something different happening on the streets. It is ugly, by our own conventional definitions, but it is still some distance away from affecting our daily lives. There is a chance it never will – unless we live in a city daft enough to host a summit. As yet, I suspect it has not influenced big business decisions, other than at the margin. But it might soon encompass both, and we should therefore seek to understand it.

I lived through the industrial relations 'wars' in British business, which was bad enough. I have witnessed first-hand the fight against racism, and other forms of discrimination, in the US – but never have I seen two 'sides' so distant in core values. The big governments and global corporations spout righteous objectivity – that we must have law and order, we must have more summits not less, more globalism not less, and that the more they talk the better off the world is and yada yada yada. They scan a world that has increasing wealth creation, relatively full employment and only a handful of localized wars. Sure, the Muslim world seems a bit pissed off, and we need to sort out that bearded guy – but only two of the 'top' fifty countries are now not democracies. Life is good. They simply do not understand why there is a sudden widespread and growing alienation.

Let me open my own kimono a bit. I'm a white, 56-year-old male. I'm pretty boring. My consistent position through life has been socially liberal and financially conservative. In short – James Dean I am not. But you know what? I am beginning to share some of the frustrations of the people on the streets.

I have never – ever – felt further away from the politicians elected to represent my interests. I am not alone – barely half the populations of the UK and US actually voted at the recent national elections, a terrifying statistic whichever side of the barricade you are on. While our 'elected' politicians pander to the vested interests of those who actually got them there, poverty and functional illiteracy grows daily in the US and the public services crumble in the UK. Add to that the growing influence of global brands, with half the world's top 100 economies now being corporations. These entities can now affect populations the size of small and medium-size countries, but show no signs of democracy. Cut through the rhetoric and they are still driven by earnings per share.

Real power in the world at large is now structured around the *pareto* principle – that 80% of power is held by 20% of the players, the latter being a mix of companies and governments. There is no great evil scheme to destroy the world, but these power-brokers are driven by their own agendas. They are the 'haves' and they want to have more. They pursue cold-eyed logic. Their gods are EVA (Economic Value Added), profits and/or market share. Governments are so myopic, sensitive to opinion polls and openly wired in to vested interests that they have become an embarrassment to the common man. None of them are driven by *balanced* interests, and it has become impossible for the ordinary folk to influence them in any way. That's why the man on the street has become so alienated – in increasing numbers.

I despair of this gap being closed. At best, I believe it will get worse before it gets better. Governments may then be forced to remember they are for the people, not just their 'investors'. Brands may also be forced to remember they exist because of their employees and customers, and not just their 'investors'. But don't hold your breath.

It sounds as though I will be an unlikely rebel, but, you know, if the light catches me just right, I look a bit like James Dean might have looked like at 56.

I wonder if I still have my old ski mask? If not, they may have one at the local charity shop.

38

'I SAY, WOULD YOU MIND AWFULLY ...'

We've established somewhere else that I love history, particularly its paradoxes. The main paradox being, of course, that I hated it at school when I had to learn it.

You can look at history through all colours of lenses. You can be depressed at the lies of omission taught today in the high schools of 'developed' society. You can be outraged at past 'values' – which saw shell-shocked 17-year-olds summarily executed as 'deserters' during World War I. You can blink, disbelieving, at a page in a history book that tells you of 'errant' slaves sawn in half, while still alive, in Jackson Square, Atlanta. You can make an objective case that Churchill should have been hanged as a war criminal in 1945.

You can also wonder what might have been if some attitudes hadn't changed so fast.

Let me give you the case of Sir Hector MacDonald, Commander of the British forces in Ceylon[1] in 1903. He was a Boer War hero, but had been disgraced, exposed as a pederast, and faced a court martial. Here's what happened to him. He was summoned back to England to have a pre-trial meeting with his Field Marshall. From that meeting, while in England, he was *'called'* to a meeting with King Edward VII. After meeting his monarch, he neatly cut the whole process short by shooting himself. This was ever so thoughtful of him.

Speculation has it that the King himself quietly suggested this solution over dinner – which is ironic, if true, because the King himself had many big appetites, only some of which were to do with food.

I can't help it. I am fascinated by why and how that meeting was staged, and how the hell King Eddie broached the subject. What do you do? Wait until the port (an 1877 Taylor's I presume?) and then lean gently forward, let the first cigar smoke clear, and amiably let it drop:

I say, old bean. What ho. Had a chat with the powers that be, and it would be awfully bad sport to let this spot of bother reach the papers. You know, the good name of the Regiment and all that. What ho. Might make sense for all parties if you topped yourself – and sooner rather than later.

I can only imagine Big Mac never blinked or skipped breath:

Absolutely, your Majesty. You took the words right out of my mouth. Great – really great – idea. Now, how about a top up of the old tawny? Some cheese? It looks an awfully good drop of Stilton.

What has this got to do with modern business? This bizarre incident reflects a time when public figures, faced with failure, were prepared

---

1 Now Sri Lanka. As pay-back for the Empire thing, they now regularly beat England at cricket.

to stand up and accept responsibility, and the ramifications that came with it. Not every one of these involved a bottle of whisky and a revolver, and not every one involved scandal. But a public failure was not necessarily seen as dishonourable in an age when honour was still worn as though it was your best suit. No, the dishonour came from *the way you handled failure*. If you openly accepted responsibility, you didn't try and deflect the blame and you stepped down from office and disappeared for a while, the chances are that you could rise again. Society at large, and your peers specifically, could forgive an honourable human failing, but they would not forgive a dishonourable attempt to lie, hide and profit from it.

Now, contrast that with today's business heroes. Recently, a whole gaggle of businesses have failed. A load of them were the dotcoms or in telecoms, and it's not the first time such a bubble has burst in history, and it won't be that last. But it has been widespread and painful. Investors have seen market values tank and some folk have lost their pensions. Employees are being laid off, again, in thousands.

Behind all this carnage are a bunch of business 'leaders', who saw nothing to worry about when their price/earnings ratios were in triple digits, their borrowings (and gearing) were off the graph, their overhead burn-rates were chomping their liquidity and their revenues a long-distant promise.

It is wrong to say their myopic leadership was solely responsible for bringing down this total house of cards, but they were on the bridges of their ships when it happened. Those who suffered when their particular companies crashed had nowhere else to look for responsibility and accountability than at the *Grande Fromage* who was leading the business at the time. Now then, have there been a bunch of honourable suicides, or – at the very least – some honourable acceptances of guilt and resignations as a result of all these failure and failing?

Naaah. Let's take the early millennium case of Richard McGinn, who supervised the disintegration of shareholder value in

Lucent (along with more than ten thousand jobs) during his three-year time on the ship's bridge. I could have picked any of 20 names, from either side of the Atlantic, (Marconi? DEG? Enron? WorldCom? Time Warner/AOL?) to make this point. Did any of them voluntarily resign? I don't think so. Quite the opposite, in some cases – they were paid huge sums to leave or trousered huge amounts before the axe eventually fell. The 'price' Mr McGinn 'charged' for jumping ship at Lucent was (approximately) $13m, and he is entitled to a long list of future perks including a near $1m annual pension.

There is no public disgrace with these people. They are hidden behind a panel of attorneys. The exit packages are all definitive agreements. Everything is legal.

After a lot of thought, I have concluded that there really is no need for these failing people to kill themselves in these sanguine and civilized times. But that may need to change soon, and my suggestion to today's business community is that somebody should *take on the role* that King Edward played, so thoughtfully, in 1903. You know the kind of thing – civilized dinners, decent port, the making of sensible and sensitive judgements, realistic solutions proposed. It would need to be somebody, as the King was, who was prepared to make an example now and again.

It would work, I know it would. I am, by coincidence, available for the role, for a small monthly retainer.

DON'T READ THIS
BEFORE YOUR
CHICKEN SOUP

I have lived a full and contributive life. It was I who brought all our children back to their senses by inventing, planning and overseeing the execution of the punk rock movement. I cannot, of course, claim full authorship – but it was I, together with a thin, wiry, bitter Elvis Costello, back in the seventies, who decided, one night, albeit after a jug or two of misty *raki,* that the Moody Blues had become too bloated and orchestrated. The rest, of course, is history. Our children were saved.

For many, that would be enough for one lifetime. Not me. Angered by the docility and comfort of the wealth-creating institutions of the eighties, I sat down with another friend, Ivan Whatshisname,[1]

1 Boesky.

and this time, helped by a decanter of fine pudding wine, we planned the whole junk-bond thing. That proved so radical that I had to call in a few IOUs in the White House and Downing Street to stay out of jail. Ivan, of course, was not so lucky.

You would think that reforming the whole youth movement and the basic structures of wealth creation would be enough – but I'm off again. This time I need to sort out these things called 'consumers'. They are becoming their own worst enemies.

I'll start with chicken, move through salmon and on to airlines. On the way I'm planning to develop a theory. Trust me.

The free market is like democracy and the Internet. The benefits of all three of them are extensive and obvious, but the pitfalls are significant and usually swept under the rug. All three of them can be defended on the basis that, *on balance*, we are much better off with them than without them.

One of the tenets of the free market is that competition will provide the required Darwinism. Supply and demand lines will cross on a graph and fix a value for a product or service. If the market is left alone, the aggregate of all those points will optimize the 'welfare' of the largest possible number of people. The problem is that the common way of measuring value is the price you pay for it, and the increasing assumption is that the cheaper it is, the better it is for the buyer. Therefore, the cheaper it is, the more you will sell of it.

Now then. This works well in areas where nobody is actually put at risk or exploited by cheapening the products. But the reality is the Hunt for Low Overhead increasingly involves exploitative practices – for example using Third World labour on rates of pay that are on or below the poverty line. In my observation it can now also involve real risks to the ignorant but enthusiastic consumer.

In my childhood we were neither rich nor poor. A roast chicken, however, was still something of an event in our post-war English house, and tasted *wonderful*. Salmon was a true rarity, costing, as it did, the price of a dozen or so alternative day-to-day meals for a pound of it. Air flights were still a dream. Today, all three are virtual commodities. On the surface, that is welcome news for the consumers of the world. It should also be terrifying.

Chicken is cheap. Why? Because, if the average reader knew the true conditions of the battery farming techniques that have been brought into play to make that cheapness possible, they would faint. I am not going to go into detail here – but it is fairly indisputable that at least 20–30 MILLION battery chickens are killed, worldwide, each day – which makes The Holocaust, Aids and other epoch-making humanitarian catastrophes minor league if we just use numbers of animate mortalities as a yardstick. They (the chickens) are killed in a none-too-pleasant way, after about six weeks of a none-to-pleasant life, at the end of which they can just stand up in the space they are allowed after being pumped with growth-promoting antibiotics. Sure it's cheap. But the only way you can get any flavour from the 'meat' is to coat it with sauce or spices.

Salmon? The 'salmon' on most of our plates today bears no relation to the athletic king of the wild stream that is the true bearer of the name. I spoke earlier of the epiphany I had when eating a fresh-from-the-river fish recently. Compare that to the natural habitat of most of the 'fish' presented to us in the name of salmon today. It is less than the equivalent of a bath full of chemically tainted, louse-and-parasite-infested, excrement-laden, and occasionally toxic, seawater. This is known as a farm. Their diet is mainly colorant. Many of them now 'escape' their prison farms and infect their wild cousins. They now threaten the very existence of the real thing. Sure it's cheap. It bloody well should be because it's virtually *ersatz* and a potential ecological disaster. I can't believe it has the same DNA grouping anymore.

It's not just food. Air travel is now within the financial reach of most people. What the year 2001 taught us, however, is that a big plane, full of fuel, in the hands of a trained pilot who has a profoundly different opinion on the sanctity of human life than most of us, is a fearful weapon. One of the reasons air flights are so (relatively) cheap, is that the security practices required to *completely* avoid those circumstances are expensive and, therefore, under-resourced. Domestic air travel in the US over the years has become as easy – and I mean that from a security point of view – as hopping on a bus.

Cheapness that involves exploitation and/or risk is not value. In my world, chicken, salmon and air travel (as a START) would cease to be commodities. They should be mandated to cost at least ten times as much as they do, and become special again. They would become special again because they could be done properly. We will then re-discover what chicken tastes like by only eating it once every month after roasting a free range bird in the oven. We will save up for, and celebrate, a piece of salmon – maybe once a year. Unaccompanied 'minors' under the age of 30 will be banned from travelling by air, and then limited to twice a year and family funerals. All three would, again, apart from the funeral trips, become things to look forward to.

All my life I have lived by simple rules. When I was a young boy, I learned that when my mum and dad had been arguing, *you should never let either of them brush your hair*. When I was a young parent, I learned *never to let a three-year-old hold a tomato*. When doing business with Scandinavians, I learned the wisdom of their old saying: *never eat yellow snow*. When I quit big business, I decided *I would forget one person a day for the rest of my life*.

I have a new one. It was resolved early in the new millennium. As of that day *I will never knowingly eat farmed salmon*. I've held it so far without a single regret.

Wow. Is there no stopping me? First, our children, and then our wealth creators. Now I've sorted out the world's consumers. Next, I will take on nurses' pay followed by the whole male jewellery thing. For the latter my ingoing position will be that *you should wear no jewellery once nose hair appears*.

IT'S LIFE, JIM – BUT NOT AS WE KNOW IT

Depending on your religious leanings, you will have different views on the origin of the Earth and life on it. Some of you will hold that it was created in a week, others that it evolved over squillions of years. You will, I believe, however, all agree on one thing – that whoever (or whatever) was responsible for it got a lot of things wrong. For example: for a project of this size and complexity there are not enough toilets or parking spaces provided.

Every now and again you do get a pleasant surprise. Purely for research purposes,[1] I found myself down in the south of France. It was all rather agreeable, and I can say, without a doubt, that the *Côte*, certainly while I was looking at it, albeit I was squinting a bit,

---

1 You have no idea how I put myself out for you all.

was certainly *d'Azur*. I had just completed a leisurely luncheon at a small bistro off the square in old Antibes (as one does at this time of year) and arrived, a little unsteadily, at our car. Somebody else was driving, I hasten to add. As I opened the door, the tight design of the French car park necessitated my door touching the door of the car parked next to it. It so happened that, at the very point of contact, the door was designed to bevel out, and was protected by a rubber strip. The other car – which was a different (and competing) brand – matched it *exactly*. They had obviously talked – and brought order where there was none.

In a time when your business should either be a tiny local niche or international, many businesses are looking beyond national boundary lines for growth. Such examples as the matching car doors – where common sense has been tied to common standards – are encouraging, but a further ten seconds of thought throws up a bunch of circumstances that highlight that the opposite is the rule rather than the exception. The world population does *not* talk to itself, and frequently fails miserably to co-align the bleeding obvious.

Here are some of my favourites:

- If you conduct a transaction on the 4th March, in the US the date is recorded as 03.04. In the rest of the world it is recorded as 04.03. This can cause confusion. If the 4th March is, for example, the expiry date of your US credit card, and somebody is checking its validity in a place that is not in the US, all hell breaks loose. I have no preference – either way is fine by me. But could somebody please pick ONE method for the planet?
- Why do we need two ways to measure temperature? Guys, water freezes at zero, not 32 degrees. If it is ten below freezing, it is minus ten, not twenty-two degrees positive.
- A4/letter-size paper varies slightly in size as you cross the Atlantic. One is marginally shorter and wider than the other. It's not a problem until you send a long fax – in either direction – to somebody who receives it on a rolled paper fax machine. Then

the pages do not match. The problem, naturally, worsens with the length of the fax. What's the big deal about moving to ONE size of paper?

- Phone lines are basically the same technical specification across the world – but you have to access wildly different jack points in the wall using a variety of adaptors. Why? Why not just pick ONE, starting NOW? In which case I state my preference for the US/International model – which is tiny. At the other end of the spectrum, I would hate it to be the French model – which means you can take one with you on your travels OR a spare pair of shoes, but not both (they are about the same size).

- We know the earth has Metric and Imperial measurement systems. And we know that a ton is nearly the same as a tonne *but not quite*. But surely, even if it is beyond the capability of our planet to move to one system, within the Imperial system itself, surely we could run with just ONE gallon? Why does a British gallon differ significantly from a US gallon? Somebody pick ONE. Please.

- Computer keyboards. It is understandable that English-based keyboards differ – to cater, for example, for different currency units. It is helpful, therefore, that software exists to enable you to change your keyboard from (say) US to UK layout. But does it have to do so via the @ sign disappearing under the ' sign, the £ appearing under the hash symbol, and the latter disappearing without trace? This only took me four weeks to figure out.

All these are ridiculous examples of unnecessary man-made barriers, and it doesn't have to be like this. As you know, many invisible hands bring order to the planet. Some of them are natural forces – the kind that mean that when you toss a coin a hundred times you will usually get about 50 heads and 50 tails, but if you drop buttered toast on the floor 100 times it will end up buttered-side down about 95 times. Some laws are absolutely inviolate: if nobody can understand why a stock value keeps rising, eventually it will fall. If it seems too good to be true it's because that's *precisely what it is*.

Some of these forces are mysterious. Here's one that intrigues me: if you measure the length of a river along all its windy bits from source to mouth, and then you measure it in a *straight line* from source to mouth, and you divide the first measurement by the second, you will, in all likelihood, get a figure not un-adjacent to 3.142. This figure, as anybody who has fought their way through school will remember, is known as π. Here's another one: apparently, and I haven't measured this personally you understand, the height of the great Pyramid of Cheops is *exactly* one billionth of the distance between the earth and the sun at their closest point. And the guys who did it probably didn't even have a ruler.

Now, I have no idea how all that stuff works, or why. None. Nada. But it shows that somebody or something *can* get an act together.

I'll finish where I started – you will all have your own ideas about the source of these mysterious powers. Let me ask a favour: if you are in personal contact with whoever it is you believe to be responsible, just ask them to take a bit of time out to fix the planet's fax paper, date recording, PC keyboards, gallon measurement, temperature measurement and phone jack points.

But do thank them for sorting out car doors. They certainly saved me a few francs.

41

PEOPLE ARE OUR GREATEST ASSET (AND OTHER CORPORATE LIES)

To Scotland, by my calculation the fifty-third country I have visited. I know many US readers will not have been there, but most will have mental images of all that wonderful traditional Scottish stuff – kilts, St Andrews golf, malt whisky, the Highlands and Mel Gibson in *Braveheart*. I fell in love with the place 25 years ago when my wife and I had a bed-and-breakfast touring holiday in the Western Isles. We were introduced to a concept called High Tea, which followed High Lunch, which itself followed High Breakfast. I put on about 40 pounds in ten days.

In the winter it's a bit of an effort for a recent Florida dweller like me to brave the climate and go there – but I was determined so to do. The event was to celebrate the winners of a bunch of prestigious corporate training awards, and I wanted to hoot and holler my support. In these parlous and difficult times, when discretionary spend budgets have all but disappeared from sight, these companies had been brave enough to write checks and raid the corporate coffers to invest in developing their people.

The images of September 11 are, of course, still horribly fresh in our minds. What happened immediately afterwards, to some degree, seems a bit blurry. There was a load of political rhetoric and military movement. Consumers changed a lot of buying habits overnight. Financial markets reflected a surge out of equities. Many companies seemed frozen in the headlights, simply – and understandably – just not sure of the implications for them. A few of them, however, moved very rapidly and within a couple of days had announced huge employee lay-offs – some of them in double digit thousands.

Now then. I'm willing to make a bet. If you took those companies who made such a move, and you scoured their recent corporate communication documents, and/or the transcripts of their recent shareholder meetings, my bet is you would find the words: *our people are our greatest asset* somewhere in there. So we have this strange pattern of behaviour – if you are suddenly faced with a crisis, you decide to face it WITHOUT your best weapon, i.e. your greatest asset.

Of course, the whole 'greatest asset' thing is a load of haggis (while I'm in Scotland …). It represents the cynicism of modern business at its worst, and has now overtaken 'empowerment' as the biggest gap between walk and talk in industry today. But I found this round of lay-offs a wee bit more sinister.

I can tell you, from experience, that mass lay-offs are complicated things to do properly. The company's behaviour and actions are, rightly, governed by employee contracts and legal regulation – which varies, sometimes by local statute as well as national law. It needs careful planning, communication and consultation. If a company announces a specific figure of x thousand lay-offs, as a reaction to a specific event, and within a couple of days of that event, it tells me that such companies were reading from one of two scripts. The first option is that the plan *already existed* in detail, and the company was actually waiting for an opportune moment, or an appropriate set of circumstances, to put it in the public domain. These would be defined, of course, as circumstances which enabled the company to blame something other than their own woeful performance for the needed cut backs. Am I saying some corporate Big Cheeses actually WELCOMED the September atrocities? Absolutely not. That would be a crass accusation. Am I saying a few took the chance to hide existing bad news behind the chaos? Absolutely.

There is another scenario – which is that a detailed plan didn't pre-exist. In which case the number of announced lay-offs had little or no science, thought or planning behind them. The eventual number probably had its genesis in a CEO banging a table and YELLING that the company needed ten thousand off the payroll. NOW. TODAY. Two days later a figure of twelve thousand (err on the side of aggression – this may not happen again) is announced – which is no more than a swish in the air in an attempt to address perceived future market slowdown and shareholder paranoia. If you can think of a better way to make the wrong decision for the wrong reason, e-mail it to me.

None of this is new. Most businesses treat employees as the accountants force us to – as expenses not assets. And I'm not daft enough to suggest that the variable cost of a company's labour force shouldn't be constantly scrutinized to make sure it is effective and efficient. Sometimes you do have to reorganize and/or restructure your business to reflect rapidly changing circumstances. And, yes, that can involve workforce reductions and it is the right decision for ALL stakeholders. What I'm saying is that we need to find a better way to live with that.

In effect, in all but a few enlightened and/or small businesses (like the ones I celebrated at the start of this column), the employee contract now represents a marriage of convenience. There is little or no loyalty either way. There is little mutual respect, love or affection. There is an understanding that one party needs the other to create respective wealth, and a secondary understanding that if either party could do without the other one, it surely would. Personally, I have no problem with that because it reflects the real world. But I would like less rhetoric and humbug to suggest something else exists when it palpably doesn't. Be honest – *our people are our greatest expense.*

Ouch. I have just tried to reread the last paragraph – and my head hurts. It's the morning after my trip to Glasgow. I am aboard an EasyJet flight heading south. The airline's credo is that they offer no food, which is a good thing. I have a head like a robber's dog, and my *hair hurts.* One thing I forgot to mention about the Scots – they know how to party.

AND SO IT CAME TO PASS
... OH NO IT DIDN'T ...

A generation ago, we entered the Age of Aquarius. I remember the moment vividly, as the cast sang about it in a controversial stage musical of the day, called *Hair*. It was controversial because the same cast took their clothes off. This nakedness lasted for precisely nine seconds (I timed it), during which time they were bathed in a blue spotlight. This made the men look very cold.

As we entered this exciting new Age, many wise people made prophecies. They examined the deep-seated trends of the day and multiplied them by the square root of the *zeitgeist*. It is amazing, as we look back now, just how *none* of them came to pass. Let's have a closer look.

We were all going to enjoy vastly more *leisure time*. Yup, the plan was that all the technology developments would enable those of us working in the developed and civilized West to cut back on working hours. The primary industries would move over to the developing nations, and we would create the same relative wealth as before by working in finance, the 'professions' or selling pizza for a couple of days a week. Our big new problem would be knowing what to do with all our new-found leisure time. People wrote books on this exciting new social challenge. Thirty or forty years later, we are still waiting for it to arrive. If anything, it looks more distant.

What happened, of course, was that the primary industries did disappear, as did large herds of administrative employees. Which left two camps of people – those who kept a job (who found themselves working longer and harder for the same money) and those who lost their jobs (who found themselves doing two or three minimum wage jobs to survive). And the Age of Aquarius was batting 0 for 1.

Now here's one that was a real banker. It was forecast that women would cease to be women and become Persons. This would have major social implications in the home, as the career woman would irrevocably change the face of family architecture. It also had huge implications for business. There would be no distinguishing women from men in the workplace, and long established discriminations would quickly erode and disappear. A quick look at the results indicates 0 for 1 becomes 0 for 2.

Let's take the two fundamental measurements – equal pay and representation at the highest decision-making levels in business. Take pay first: at micro level, on both sides of the Atlantic, each woman's pay level can be justified up the Wahoo as equal. It has to be, legally. But guess what? At macro level, when you add up their total pay as a race of Persons, and then average it out, they are still behind. As for boardroom representation, a scan of the top executive positions in the Fortune or FTSE list of blue chip companies shows an alarming stereotype when it comes to key executives – white, male, somewhere around 50 years old and with a bucketful of stock options. This is probably the most boring, unadventurous, conservative with a small 'c' demographic on the planet. If they have any hair it is almost universally parted where their daddy parted it about 45 years ago. And these are the folk *in charge*.

Oh, and while we are at it, the similar prophesies that disabled people and minorities would also make progress, and similarly become Persons, has also lost a wheel when it comes to boardroom and senior management representation.

Now here's a prophecy that surely must have come good – that we would all become far healthier. The constant whining of do-gooders, the overdose of information on what's good and bad for you, the ready availability of nutritious food all the year round at affordable prices, and the carpet bombing of the media with photographs of what you *should* look like and articles on how you *should* live was irresistible, *n'est-ce pas*? Er, no. Highly resistible, actually. Obesity is rising, more kids smoke, fewer kids exercise, the volume of alcohol intake may be down but the strength of the average drink is up – and soft drugs are marginally less common than cheese crackers. During my time on the bridge of the good ship Burger King, in response to this projected new trend, we tested putting low-fat mayo on the Whopper hamburger. For a week or two I was on the FBI's most wanted list. So that's 0 for 3.

Aha!!! But what about telecommuting, I hear you ask? That was forecast, and that surely happened, didn't it? Thousands of administrative workers, previously glued to a chair in a cubicle, would now have the freedom to work in their jimjams. They would be able to link seamlessly with their Korean suppliers or their German customers while applying ointment to little Billy's zits. Er, no, actually. That not only hasn't happened, it shows no sign of turning up. Less than *one half of one percent* of the eligible workforce now telecommute. It would seem that either they don't like it, or the company doesn't like it, or (my theory) both of them dislike it. I can understand both points of view: for many workers there is actually an *attraction* about leaving the house and having another life with another bunch of people. Sure, they'd like a better balance, with more time at home

– but not the Full Monty. As for employers, the benefits of having your people together are perceived to still outweigh the potential real estate savings. Age of A? 0 for 4.

Poor old Age of Aquarius – but I still love it. One of its attractions is that it has fooled us all. I grew up with an Iron Curtain across Europe – and it has completely gone. Quite unbelievable – along with many other unpredictable developments. Of course, I don't like all that has happened – from the failure of the forecast breakthrough of women into the boardroom, to the nightmare of global terrorism.

On balance, though, it's a wonderful Age, and we should celebrate it. It has certainly taught me some valuable lessons. I will never, for example, remove my clothes if there is a blue light on. And certainly not if I'm singing at the time.

DANGER!
GENIUS AT WORK

I hit the entrance to Big Business in the 1970s, armed only with a pair of flared trousers and an MBA. As I remember it, the trousers were the colour of a respectable claret, and of a decent quality. They lasted a few months before I discarded them, moving on to the safety pins and rags of punk rock. The MBA, however, only lasted a week or two.

It only took that long to realize that all that fancy stuff was no use in the real world of business. Whenever I mentioned regression analysis people would blush and turn away – as though I had left my flies undone. For a short period, I could actually write computer programs in a thing called Fortran. This proved quite the most useless skill I ever inherited, beating by a short head my uncanny ability to forget names within 24 hours.

As I progressed, rather like Eddie The Eagle in reverse, up the ladder of Big Business, I found my inspiration in other sources. Strangely, the higher I got, the more the works of some of the great philosophers played a part. When I reached the shores of the USA, captaining the good ship Burger King, I found that the Stoic school of thinking was suddenly appropriate – summarized here as: *'Things will be Bad. For Christ's sake plan on that basis.'* Later, my leadership became inspired by the ideas of the gloomy German philosopher, Hegel, again summarized here for your benefit as: *'You are born wet, hungry and crying. Then it gets worse.'* Both these came in handy when dealing with the Burger King franchisees. Trust me.

Over the last few years I have cheered up a bit. Trying to figure out what I wanted to be when I grew up (I'm only 56), I read a book by Charles Handy called *The Empty Raincoat*. In it, he outlines his thoughts – on how the basic structure of the lives of business people have changed in the last generation. It used to be three stages: dependency, job, dependency. These stages were, of course, followed by the Big Finish, i.e. death. Now, it is more likely to be a four-stage process – dependency, job, *something else*, dependency, and then the Grim Reaper.

Many folk are now finding that their basic 'careers' are over – either by their choice or somebody else's – by the time they are 50. They are also living longer. There is, therefore, a big 'gap' to fill, which previous generations never had to think about. I'm right slap bang in it, and loving it. I'm having so much fun, I can't stand it.

It's not a big jump to move that thinking on and to align it with another 'life model' theory – again, relatively new. This idea suggests that modern life is like filling a glass with stones. You start with big ones, but you can only get one or two in (main career? main relationship?). When you can't get any more big ones in, you start filling it with smaller ones. Finally, when no more of this size will go in, you finish filling the glass up to the rim with grains of sand.

That's the model I'm following, and I'm at the stage where I'm finding a whole variety of mid-sized stones and jamming them in my glass. It's stuff I'd never contemplated while I was working on the Big Stone phase.

Now then. It was only when I'd had my fifth beer that I realized we might have invented a viable business model here. This actually works for the development of many businesses (in general) and brands (in particular).

Let's take my old favourite, Burger King, as an example. The business and the brand were both born in the 1950s, and the founding geniuses, Jim McLemore and Dave Edgerton, filled the glass with big stones almost at once. The Whopper flagship sandwich, the chain broiler and the 'Have it your way' sandwich-making process were in place from the start. Fifty years on, these three still make up the basic building blocks of the system. On the journey, of course, many more 'stones' were added to the glass, although it is arguable that none of them matched the size and significance of those original three. Drive-thrus came along, as did breakfast, chicken-based products, international development, bundled up value meals and kids marketing programmes – all these, in my mind, making up the mid-sized stones. Dotted around these have been countless marketing initiatives, new product launches, re-organizations, kitchen developments and so on – which form the grains of sand.

What this theory tells us is that the big, structural elements that give a brand or a business sustainable distinction are *usually in place very early* – but that the journey doesn't stop there. There is room to add smaller stuff around the main elements, which enables you to get nearer fulfilling the real potential. And when you are tapped out with those, you can still add the grains of sand – almost *ad infinitum*.

Just stand back for a minute and look at your own business. Whether it be large or small, it is likely that the Big Idea came at the start, and if you have survived this far, that BI proved distinct and sustainable. Not one BI, however, has stood the test of time without being added to and developed. Even the daddy of 'em all, Coca-Cola, has seen can and fountain technology developments, the introduction of Diet Coke and a ton of smaller initiatives being added to its 'glass' over the years.

Where does your business stand? What's needed? More mid-sized stones? Or are you down to tweaking by adding grains of sand? *The bad news is that there is no do-nothing choice.* Nobody survives on cruise control today.

I honestly feel that this breakthrough in business modelling may warrant a Nobel Prize of some kind, an honour for which I am long overdue. There is, however, one flaw in my brilliant theory, which is causing me concern. It relates to my two sons. They actually started their lives filling their 'glasses' with sand, they have stayed with sand, and, it would seem, intend to stay with sand. Their message to me, written in sand, is: *Sand is cool. So, dad, shove your theory where the sun don't shine.*

THAT WAS THE WEEK
THAT WAS

We great writers stand accused of two crimes against humanity. First: when we are excited by an idea we often witter on for ages in pursuit of a full stop. Second: we whinge a lot. I'm currently in the latter mode.

Here's the problem. You will be reading this quite some time after I've written it. This normally precludes me writing about anything too date-specific. Frankly, there's nothing worse than reading stuff that can only see its shelf life in the rear view mirror. Two things happened during a recent week, however, that are giving me an excuse to break the rule. So please bear with me.

The week was the second week in February, 2002. During that week, we saw Kenneth Lay, late of Enron, holding up his hand in front of members of the elected government of the US and hiding behind his mum's apron – whoops, I mean the Fifth Amendment. His position was, if I have got this right, that none of it was his fault, he was innocent, everybody else guilty and *if only* his lawyers would let him testify, everybody would see that. His lawyers, however, had studied his position in detail and told him, probably wisely, to shut the fuck up.

Sometimes, to quote the immortal Stephen Fry, there just isn't enough vomit in the world.

In the same week, Anita Roddick lost control of her business. She is a less well-known personality in the US, but has legend status in the UK. By legend, I mean that nobody has no opinion about her. She was the founder and, until the week in question, the principal conductor of one of the world's best-known brands: The Body Shop.

So, we witnessed the simultaneous fall of two business leaders. What made it doubly interesting was that they represented two entirely different styles of leadership.

You don't want to get me started on Lay and his henchmen, but for debate purposes let's just say they represent the Adam Smith/Darwinist/free market/Gordon Gekko/greed is good/everybody wins if everybody pursues their own vested self interest/exploitative/overstated profit and trumped up balance sheet/share-price driven version of capitalist leadership.

Anita, on the other hand, rowed a different boat. Profit, personal greed and (unfortunately) investor returns were all low priorities on her wish list. She saw 'her' business as a vehicle that would drive the world to a better place. The cynics would have it that The Body Shop was simply an exercise *in extremis* of Cause-Related Marketing – but her consistent track record shows she sought to use 'her' business to lighten Third World oppression and ease the battering that the environment is taking from our presence. In addition, she used her own high business profile to support worthy non-business causes. She epitomized the model that recognizes that a business needs to reflect the interests of many stakeholders.

Both these fell from grace in the same week. It is as though Robin Hood went down at the same time as the Sheriff of Nottingham. Which raises the question – just where do we point our children when they ask for business leadership role models?

The defining moment for becoming 'old' for a male is when you first save a piece of wood to stir paint with in the future. I have been doing that a lot recently. Now, has age brought me wisdom, particularly in this contentious area? It certainly has.

My views on this subject are now geometrically in line with those of Mort Meyerson. Mort was, you will remember, a kind-of joint commander of the business giant EDS, together with that strange little ET-like creature who nearly became president of the US. Together they espoused a sternly protestant style of leadership, but that is not what has inspired this reference. I am much more impressed with Mort's magazine article from a couple of years back. Its contents are summarized in its title: *Everything I Thought I Knew About Leadership Is Wrong.* Bingo.

In truth, that's where most of us are. The whole leadership thing has got so complex, and brings so much pressure, that about 95% of all our preconceived ideas are capable of being proved wrong. Leaders we admire as lions crash and burn in just the same way as those we think of as donkeys. All bets are off.

You will note I said 95%. Floating about in the 5%, where we can retain some confidence, are a couple of leadership 'must-haves' that not only still survive but seem to me to be increasing in importance. They are not new and they are not fancy, but my advice is not to leave your leadership home without them.

The first is personal integrity. I cannot see *any* leadership model today that is built on deceit surviving over anything but the short term. Unfortunately the potential short-term returns can be so high that there will be those who will just go for it, but there will be fewer hiding places in future. Whether it is an exercise in 'supporting' your share price, or simply dealing with your employees, customers or affected outside parties – you will get found out today if you try and deceive. You will not necessarily be tumbled by regulation, auditors or GAAP. These bodies are all capable of missing this stuff, particularly if there is a whiff of money in the air. But there is simply too much information available that cannot be hidden all the time from all the people who sing from a different hymn sheet.

The second leadership must-have is to learn from the Orient. In the east, *a good deal is where both parties leave the table smiling.* A four or five on the dice *for both parties* is OK, it doesn't have to be six for one and a zero for the other every time. So – deal something back. Reinvest in a partnership. Surprise a customer by giving something away proactively and/or without pressure. Don't rape suppliers just because you can. Treat your employees as assets, not expenses. When you look outside your tent, show the world you give a damn.

None of this means you turn into Mother Theresa. To be an effective modern leader you cannot build just on the cornerstones of popularity and being a nice guy. But as businesses become more complex and big, the leader's role will become less and less about technical competence and more about illustrating what the company stands for.

Anita Roddick's fade-out reminds us that the *prime* purpose of being in business remains the capture and retention of a customer, and not putting the world to rights. It can have a whole bunch of secondary purposes, but if it ignores the primary one, it won't be around to deliver the sub-goals. But you can succeed without deceit and without having to take the whole pot at every visit to the table.

I know, I know – such wisdom from one so young. But the world is full of new 'wisdoms'. Another one that the new millennium has taught us all is that you are not actually a millionaire until you have sold the stock and paid the taxes.

GO ON, SURPRISE ME
– MAKE MY DAY

Despite the fact that the last 25 years has seen an alarming increase in the number of things about which I know nothing, I try and steer a course in life that avoids surprises. I follow Leibowitz's law, for example – which states that *when hammering a nail you will never hit a finger if you hold the hammer with both hands.*

Life does, of course, insist on throwing occasional spanners in the works. Only yesterday, to give you another working example, I opened a tin that clearly said 'Evaporated Milk' on the label only to find it was *still there.* In general, however, I avoid the stresses caused by events not following a predetermined script.

It was only recently that I realized that this approach might be the cause of me missing out – and that a life-plan which drifted towards the other end of the spectrum might also provide an effective and efficient business tool.

The setting for this epiphany was a restaurant in Florida. Two of us were eating, and were some way through a meal that was – as planned – unsurprising. The place was thinly populated, but there was nothing in the food, ambience, décor or service that had so far generated any sort of comment – either of praise or criticism. All that was about to change. We were positioned near the kitchen door, which slowly opened. A guy in a dark suit walked through into the restaurant area. Without any drama he approached our table and asked us how the meal had been. In fairness, we both had to think as the whole experience had been singularly unmemorable, but when it all came back to us it seemed to be OK, so we passed on the good news. His brow furrowed. Barely controlling his emotions, he startled us with a short, but memorable, speech: 'It may have seemed OK, but let me assure you I am not happy with anything in this place tonight. It does not come up to my standards. The meal is on the house.' With that he turned heel and headed off towards the next occupied table – leaving us open mouthed, and not a little worried about what we had just eaten.

After a lot of post-match analysis, and having survived the night with no negative side effects, we decided that we were a lot more impressed than concerned. It seems we had dined at a restaurant run by the last person on earth that was both honest and uncompromising – and who was prepared to lose unnecessary money in the pursuit of both. What a surprise. A pleasant one.

It's this Pleasant Surprise thing that got me thinking. Most of us would confess to a natural dislike of being surprised, but what we mean of course is *unpleasantly so*. That attitude arises because that's all we ever get. The world is now geared to bland uniformity via the spread of global brands. The whole idea of brand is to remove the element of surprise. Add to that the fact that the whole business universe is also involved in a master plan to *lower our expectations* so that we are not unpleasantly surprised every two minutes. Here's how this works in, say, the airline business. If you book a plane fight, for example, you might see a take-off scheduled at 10.15am and an arrival at 12.45pm. When you eventually take off, however, the pilot tells you that the flight time will be one hour and fifteen minutes. So, what's with the 'missing' time? By my calculation, the flight time allowed is two and a half hours. But their whole act is so crappola that they need this to cover for routine inefficiencies in their own operations, with air traffic control and in and around the start and finish airports involved. In this way, if you plan around their published times, you get no unpleasant surprises. If they do have a tail wind and arrive at the gate at 12.40pm – i.e. 'five minutes early'– you think you've won a minor prize in the Lottery.

And it's not just airlines. They are ALL doing it, trust me. Try ringing up the phone company and navigating your way through the hold-menu. Try calling a plumber. Have you ever tried to *correspond* with a big private or public sector organization? The whole process is shaped to lower your expectations to a level where you get no unpleasant surprises. Occasionally, if they do something half-right, you are anaesthetized to such a degree that you believe you have beaten the system and are pleasantly surprised.

Let's go back to our troubled restaurant manager (or owner), and see if he's unknowingly come up with a business weapon we could all use – one which is also efficient, effective and cheap. I think he has.

The key is that what he did was not just a pleasant surprise, but that it was also *proactive.* No only did he surprise us pleasantly – part of the effectiveness was that it happened *before* we were expecting anything. It came from right out of the blue and was mighty powerful. So, let's call it the PPS – the Pleasant Proactive Surprise.

It doesn't have to be expensive, and it doesn't have to be related to something going wrong. One of the most successful franchisees we had in my time with Burger King was Manny Garcia in south Florida. Sure, he had good locations and a reasonably wealthy market – but so did many others. I'm not daft enough to put his overall success just down to a couple of tiny PPSs – but his staff used to go round the restaurants with free coffee fill-ups and mints, and there was enough positive feedback from that alone which convinced me that it contributed. Here's the power of what I am talking about – the PPS is *so rare* in modern business life, it's actually exhilarating when you get one. What's important is that you do tend to go back to a business that gives you such an experience. As any marketing fule kno – once you have created awareness and generated a trial purchase, the REAL trick is to get the customer back again (raising frequency) and then hook 'em (achieving loyalty). There are few more effective and efficient ways of getting the last two than a smattering of PPSs.

It's a powerful weapon because nothing surprises us any more. We are almost anaesthetized to anything this all-shook-up world can throw at us. Here's an example: if I told you there are twice as many plastic flamingos in south Florida than real ones, you wouldn't be at all surprised would you?

Amazingly, you would be correct not to be.

THE DEFENCE SPEAKS

I belong to an elite club. Membership consists of ex-CEOs of Burger King. At the last count there were only 175,397 of us still alive.

As Club VP for External Relations, I have a responsibility. The fast food industry has recently come under heavy mortar fire from a journalist by the name of Eric Schlosser, in his book *Fast Food Nation* (Houghton Mifflin, 2001). We need a response.

In no particular order of priority, the industry stands accused of fuelling mass obesity, losing a better way of life, exploiting labour and consumers (particularly children in both camps), abusing power, being pathetically regulated, advancing new diseases, unfairly distributing wealth and over-globalizing the planet. After reading it I felt like Pol Pot.

What an absolute crock.

I couldn't attempt a detailed debate in a few paragraphs. That's even if I wanted to – and I don't. The truth is that there is much about the industry that should give everybody in it cause for concern, and objective challenge should be *welcomed*. But a full debate needs two added dimensions that the book doesn't provide.

First, it needs balance. In and of itself, the book is a powerful piece of scholarship – but in my observation a piece of work is better if the conclusions come after the research. In this case there is the very strong feeling that the author's mind was set and that the extensive research was an exercise in finding and selecting stuff to support that position.

Any industry that provides work and affordable food for many millions of people *every day*, that creates wealth, that is consistent and relatively safe and that is regulated in the main by elected governments *cannot be all bad*. That's all missing, and what the book also fails to do is to define the alternatives. Presumably they are omitted because they only exist someplace over the rainbow.

The second issue I have with Schlosser's thesis is that it addresses the symptoms, not the disease. The problem with this planet is that its population has forward momentum. People keep inventing things. People want more for themselves. The strong exploit the weak because they can do. These forces drive societal and economic changes, which bring a lot of benefits. And a lot of costs. The Internet is, perhaps the best example of all. It is wonderful – but it empowers paedophiles and bomb makers, and we have absolutely no idea how to handle that. The industrial revolution created enormous wealth and benefits – but it ruined village life and signalled the death of the craftsman. Technology has probably benefited everybody on earth – but lost millions of 'conventional' jobs en route. Sure, it would be nice to pick and choose – but you can't. The momentum is always forward. The benefits always come, but then we are all faced with managing the costs whether we like it or not.

Schlosser is right. There are some aspects of the fast food industry that are hideous and which cannot be defended. But they are not specifically about fast food. They are about the cost of the planet's development momentum and the imperfections of its population. Some examples:

- Abuse of juveniles as employees? There are regulations with which society feels comfortable, and there will be more. The real abuse comes from those little Hitlers who use their local power to run their operations like something out of Dickens. They abuse regulations and people because they can get away with it, and they exist in *every* industry. They have always existed, and unless (your) God has a plan that nobody yet knows about, they always will.
- Abuse of children as consumers? When I was a kid, you could have marketed to me till the cows came home. If my parents didn't think it was right for me, it was off limits. The crass abdication of parental responsibility is a society-wide disease. Burger King Kids Club is not the real problem here, trust me.
- Obesity? In Europe and the USA alone more than 500 million people need 2–3 meals a day. The fast food industry makes millions of meals available at affordable prices. If they didn't, I don't know who else would. It is a GOOD thing that it is there as an option. Now then, it is no big secret that some foods you eat during a week have different dietary properties. Some folk eat too much, have too many meals and have the wrong mix in their diet. Is this really a supply-side problem? No. So, eat less and/or eat better you fat bastards. It is an *entirely* discretionary consumer decision.
- Low wages? Whether the minimum wage is where it is now, or twenty times higher, or *doesn't exist at all*, there will always be a bunch of jobs in society that are (by definition) at the bottom of the pay league. They are defined by where consumer supply and demand, and labour market supply and demand, all come together at one point on society's welfare graph. And, yes, fast food is there with a group of others. But guess what? It is not

entirely a bad thing. It provides a wealth of opportunities for the low skilled and itinerant. It provides an entry point for those who can and want to develop. It has helped millions of students make ends meet on a journey that otherwise might have been impossible. And for those (like me) who are lucky enough to progress in life, it provides a workplace experience that *should* make you a more empathetic and sensitive manager of those less fortunate.

- There's just too much of it and its taking over the world? It seems to me that the fastest-growing population segment on the planet could be categorized as *nannies* – folk who assume some god-given right to look after us, who know better than us and must occasional give us a smack for misbehaving. Fast food is NOT a modern phenomenon. Wander around a market in Istanbul, and the stalls are selling appetising, hot, nutritious meals at low prices that are served and eaten quickly. Fast food has thousands of manifestations, and has been part of our way of life for centuries. Even the global brands that take the heavy hits in this book have been around for half a century. And guess what? You can't fool all the people all of the time. In my observation, almost every fast food customer knows that there are probably better ways to eat, and that fast food should not be a dominant part of a balanced diet. But it works for them, and millions upon millions of people have shown what they want over the years. It's called market demand, and you are on very dangerous ground telling so many people who have demanded so much of it for so long that they are idiots.

- Fast food supply chain processes are now all about quantity not quality? Somewhere over the rainbow there is a world where, every day, the mother of the family goes to the market, which is possibly French, early in the morning and hand picks the morning's ingredients – and spends the rest of the day in the kitchen with a mortar and pestle, slow cooking a casserole of fresh meat, vegetables and herbs. Yeah, right. For the urban and developed world this is not an option. But that world still needs feeding – an appropriate amount, at an appropriate cost and over an appropriate timescale. That needs supply chains with mind boggling logistics, mass production facilities and a zillion points of production. That's what we demand, and that's what we've got.

Schlosser had 288 pages. I've got loads more ammo, but I'll stop now. Fast food ain't the real problem. Schlosser's the real problem – inasmuch as he exists on the planet with six billion peers. I don't know the guy – but let's assume his family has, let's say, a couple of cars. Oil is the biggest polluter on earth – much bigger than fast food by any measurement. Let's assume he drinks coffee – coffee is the second biggest polluter on earth. *We are all at fault, we are all guilty.* Our aspirations and needs create demand forces that wreck the bloody planet, and are usually supplied by people. As such they are occasionally subject to greed and abuse, and occasionally out of control.

If we could cure those diseases, it would be an historic first. Meanwhile, it's a wonderful world with a lot of faults. We could and should try to do better. That is exactly what my first school report said, and it pisses me off greatly to receive the same message from a journalist some 50 years later.

I haven't had one for years, but I suddenly feel like a Whopper.

ACROSS THE GREAT DIVIDE

I am staring across at the *enemy*. The tension is such that I forget to mix my butter into my honey before I spread it on my warm fresh bread for breakfast. While I figure it all out, I take a sip of my Turkish coffee. The effect is like being hit, high on the inner thigh, with a four iron.

The 'Great Divide' I am staring across is the Bosporus Sea, the thousand metre-wide strip of water that splits the city of Istanbul. More importantly, it is the geographic border between Europe and Asia. Even more importantly, it has become the symbolic checkpoint between two worlds – the world of Islam and The West.

Ever widening over the last half millennium, since the nightmare of September 11 the gap has widened again – this time exponentially. As far as my immediate location is concerned, of course, the gap is nonexistent. The people and culture are actually the same on both banks of the water in this noisy wonderful city. They are also mostly Islamic, so I can conveniently report on all of them as the 'enemy'.

Here's my first problem. They are delightful. Busy and bustling, they have time for everybody and a constant ready smile. The women fall into two categories – 'Miss World finalists' and 'Other'. All the men try to look like Elvis at some stage in his life. And they are so nice.

Where did this all East–West thing go wrong? How and why did the Western world alienate the Muslim world on the journey? It is true that for a variety of reasons, over the last 500 years or so, the world of Islam has felt increasingly distanced from, and short changed by, the West. If I take a deep breath I can just about summarize these reasons in 54 words. Here goes:

- Islam is naturally inward looking.
- The opening of the great sea routes killed the Spice Roads.
- The New World benefited only Europe.
- The industrial revolution and the Islamic anti-science stance did the same.
- The emancipation of women has allowed the full species to develop in the west.
- Islam never separated Church and State.

As the gap was widening, the three forces that could have helped narrow it – politics, religion and international commerce – actually worked in the opposite direction. Nobody should be surprised about the first two of those – throughout history they have contributed far more than anything else to the planet's misery and division. But you would have hoped, maybe, that the explosion of international business, driven (initially) by the West in the last couple of hundred years, might have had a more uniting effect on the planet. Not so.

In the early days, of course, the pioneering international capitalists didn't have to justify anything. They operated on the same motto as British royalty – never apologize, never explain. They simply exploited foreign raw materials, labour and markets – sometimes in the most brutal rapine way. Over the last few decades, of course, companies have had to put narratives in their annual reports, and signal signs of caring, justification and conscience. But nothing has really changed.

The West still pontificates that global business can be an agent for positive change and increased unity. It preaches that deregulated 'free' trade can help to blend the East and West – and get the best of both worlds. But what we really want is the continuation of the status quo. We want our brands in their markets and access to their cheap labour. We even have a vested interest in their cycles of war and poverty – we sell them weapons for the first and food for the second. Of course, we call the second one 'aid' – but they pay a price when they read the terms and conditions. Should they get too buoyant, we shield our chronic balance of payment deficits by protection.

Now and again, we really go over the top to let them know who is still boss. The world will never forget – rightly so – the horrific events of September 11. The (Western) world has almost forgotten, however, the events of Bhopal, when the US-based Union Carbide Corporation accidentally slaughtered *thirty thousand* Indians – and maimed a multiple of that number. Nobody has been hunted down for those consequences and compensation was eventually a dollar short and many days too late for most of the victims. The company chairman has gone into lifelong hiding. Sure there is a difference – one was deliberate and one was only negligent – but if that had been an Iranian company operating in Texas or Surrey, how would we all have felt? Not a huge amount differently from September 11, I warrant.

Political and religious leaders will never narrow this gap. It is against their self-interest to do so. But business could still contribute enormously to the people of this planet coming together. Cultural differences should be kept and celebrated, but we have to start again in many things. We need to stop encouraging their war and poverty cycles. Instead of selling weapons and loans, we need to invest in their technical research programmes and infrastructure. Sure, it's great for us in the West when they build a McDonald's in Istanbul, but – if you define fast food as quickly served and/or quickly eaten and not necessarily quickly prepared – they have the finest fast food in the world. Let's have 30,000 of their wonderful food stalls in our markets.

When you met these folk as ordinary people, they are a delight – and enough goodwill is created to light up a town. Time and again I reflect that it's only when we let bad leaders actually lead it all goes pear shaped. Staying in a hotel close by us are two American ladies, neither of whom will see seventy again. They have chosen to ignore the advice given to travellers by the US government – which is not to travel 'east of Venice'. By the by, it is a long time since I have heard advice given to anybody, on anything, that is as fatuous, nannying and myopic – and it is to the credit of this astonishing duo that they have treated it with the disdain it deserves. They are a sheer delight to be around, making notes on everything, chattering away using their increasing Turkish vocabulary, showing an insatiable appetite to learn and understand as much as they can about the people and the place. Their approach is not just about meeting halfway. It is not about 'us' and 'them'. It is about 'we'. It takes two old ladies to hammer home to me that there are six billion of us on this planet, and we need to get closer not further apart.

On behalf of all of us in the West, I am embarrassed at my reticence, distance and inadequacy. Since I have arrived, I have mastered about two words of Turkish – simply because I can't be arsed. Between them, these two women weigh less than me, and probably couldn't lift a rifle, but what inspiring role models. Wouldn't it be wonderful to see real people like that lead the world of business, politics and religion?

Later, I jump on the ferry and travel all the way to Asia. Just for lunch. It takes all of 20 minutes to sail in the sun across the Great Divide. As I relish my lamb with spinach, and contemplate a sweet cake for dessert, I reflect that this is an awfully pleasant way to sleep with the enemy.

AND NOW FOR SOMETHING COMPLETELY DIFFERENT

With a start I realize it is almost a decade since I left my position as the Anna Kournikova of Big Business. From the minimal research I have done on the subject, it seems nobody missed me. Few people, apart from my bank manager, evidenced any distress at the time. Had he been actually dead, he assured me, he would have accorded me the honour of turning in his grave.

I have never missed that world for a minute. Others who have left it have felt the need to justify the move – 'wanting to spend more time with the family' being a favoured reason. I simply decided that, after a quarter century of bosses sticking foreign bodies up my rectum, I would never work for anybody again.

I have survived, without the covering fire of a big corporation and a paycheck, thanks to the rigid application of a three-part formula I designed at the time. The three elements are deceptively simple: a) make a lot of lists; b) forget one person every day and c) track nothing but cash flow. It was only with the wisdom afforded by ten years hindsight that I realized that if I had applied these rules while I was a Big Cheese I would have been a far better CEO. Let me expand.

It was Tom Peters, I think, who said 'If you've got more than one priority you got none'. Forgetting the massacre of what we used to know as English, this always struck me as sound advice. I followed it, as I know thousands of other managers did and still do. Today, however, I start every day with a new Post-It note, listing at least twenty tiddly things with which I must occupy my time. Some days I have two lists. Some days I have *lists of lists*. I suddenly realized that this is actually a magnificent way to run a business – because having the Single Great Big Priority from Hell is now far too inflexible for modern needs. Business is so multi-dimensional and fast-changing, my new way is the ONLY way to map your journey. Besides, if you have no real idea about your priorities, your competitors won't have a clue. This is now the only way to stay ahead of the market. Also, if you can change priorities in a heartbeat, and actually forget or even *lose* some, you can avoid the SMEF (Spontaneous Massive Existence Failure), which is so popular among many of today's global giants.

Next one? This is a lot more subtle. *Forget one person everyday*. I invented this because of worries about my memory. I have an outstanding ability to remember the names of all the Kinks, but an outstanding inability to remember somebody I met yesterday. Clearly, I am heading for short-term memory troubles in my later years, so this tactic was devised to *get there first*. In this way, I will be in control. So, I work hard, and deliberately sit down and forget somebody every day. *Eureka!* I found I had stumbled on *another* winning management strategy. We all know far too many people, and constantly try to remember more. We have far too many acquaintances and not enough relationships. We (particularly males) need to stop flannelling, and trying to impress. We need to figure out who is important to us, and to whom we mean something special. The reality in modern business is that there are about 15 people who are personally mission-critical to most of us. These are the relationships that need working and nurturing. One by one, you should forget the rest. You will see things much more clearly, and you will be sure-footed and pleasant to be with.

Finally? *Ignore everything else – just track the cash.* I was given advice once by a veteran in the brewing industry when I was head-hunted for a job he thought he should have landed. Effectively, I ended his career by being brought in over his head. He still had the grace and class to try and help me. He told me that if anybody wanted to learn about a business quickly they should sign every business check and read every paying-in slip for a couple of weeks. I ignored it then, but recognize it now for a jewel of advice. I run my life now on a cash-accounting basis – and if I ever rejoined Big Business I would monitor little else. One of the fundamental cancers in business now is the ability to lie, through and over (and in some cases abetted by) auditors, and present GAAP accounts which actually show what the profits would have been if the company hadn't paid its bills or invested in e-commerce. The ONLY solution is for the world to move to cash accounting for its primary presentation of results, with all the other crappola attached as appendices. Forget paper valuations and non-cash items. Forget the difference between balance sheets and operating statements. If you've spent it, it's gone. If you've received it, you can use it. Nothing else matters.

There is a possibility that I have completely revolutionized the combined science and art of business management with these discoveries. There may be a book – and possibly a film, even a mini-series, in it for me. All I can say is that they work for me, and I wish I'd thought of them 25 years ago. You might want to give 'em a go.

Now then. I can see there are the sceptics among you who believe I am pulling everybody's leg. You are tempted to think that this exciting new approach to management is just a joke to fill a couple of blank pages on a morning so far noticeable only for my writers block.

The only way I will dignify such comments with a response is to echo Peter Cooke's wonderful speech to Dudley More in the film *Bedazzled*. Looking (as ever) marginally more enigmatic than the Mona Lisa, Cooke uttered the immortal words: 'Everything I have told you so far is a complete lie. Including that.'

Which might be a good note on which to finish.

INDEX